FOR ORGANS, PIANOS & ELECTRONIC KEYBOARDS

E-Z PLAY TODAY

106

20 TOP HITS

ISBN 978-1-4950-0786-6

HAL•LEONARD® CORPORATION

7777 W. BLUEMOUND RD. P.O. BOX 13819 MILWAUKEE, WI 53213

Visit Hal Leonard Online at
www.halleonard.com

CONTENTS

The A Team

Registration 4
Rhythm: Folk or Ballad

Words and Music by
Ed Sheeran

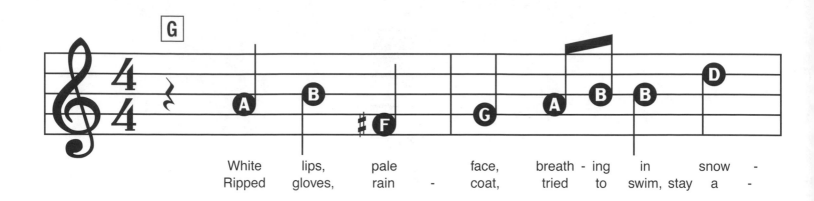

White lips, pale face, breath - ing in snow -
Ripped gloves, rain - coat, tried to swim, stay a -

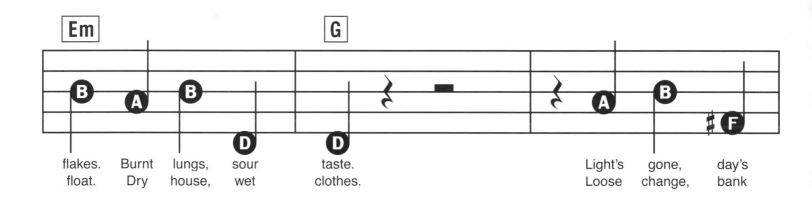

flakes. Burnt lungs, sour taste.
float. Dry house, wet clothes.
Light's gone, day's
Loose change, bank

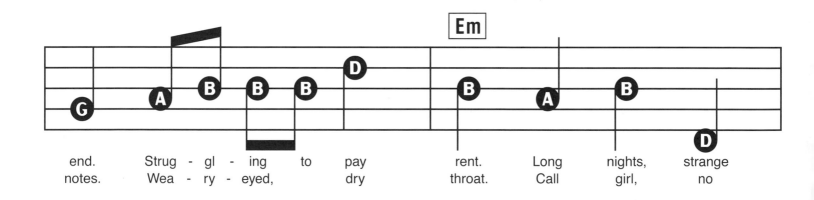

end. Strug - gl - ing to pay rent. Long nights, strange
notes. Wea - ry - eyed, dry throat. Call girl, no

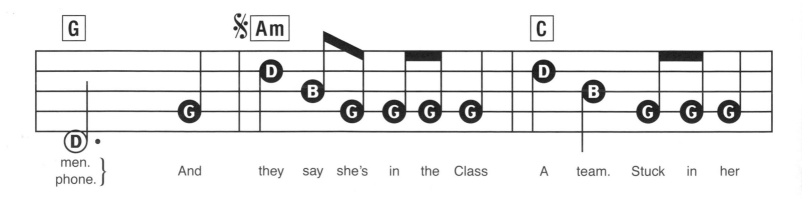

men.
phone.
And they say she's in the Class A team. Stuck in her

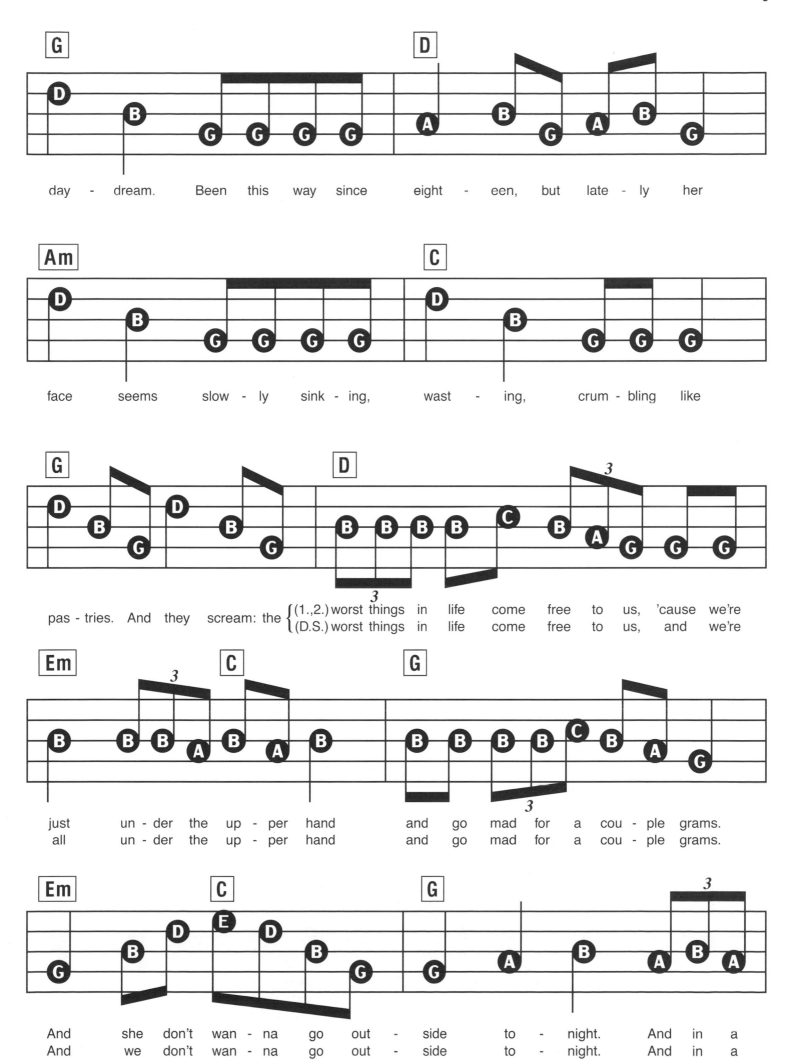

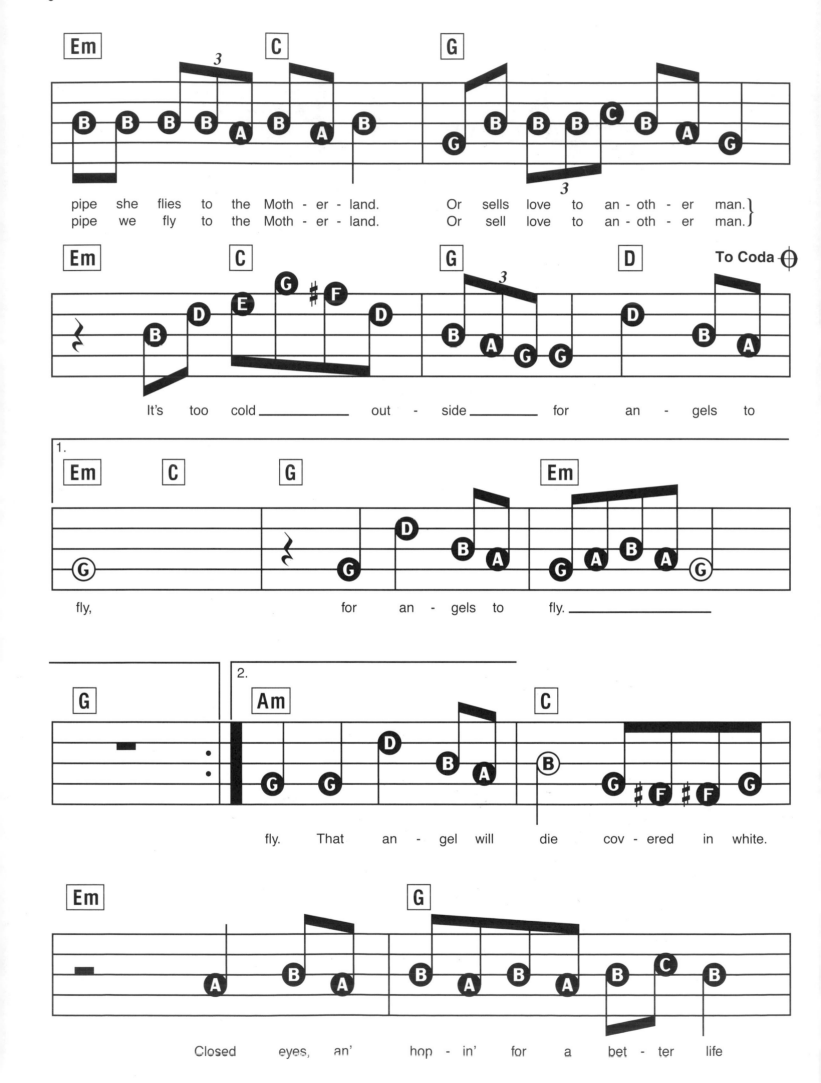

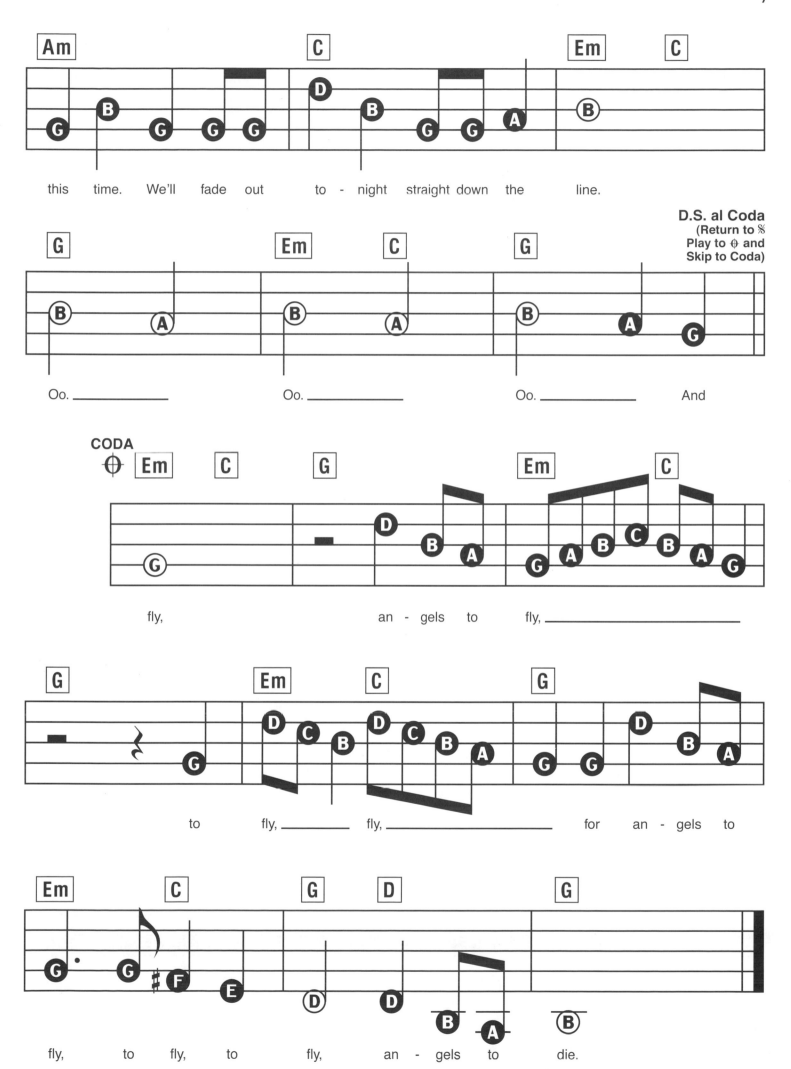

All of Me

Registration 8
Rhythm: Ballad

Words and Music by John Stephens
and Toby Gad

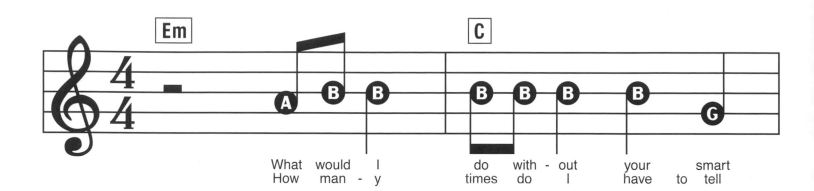

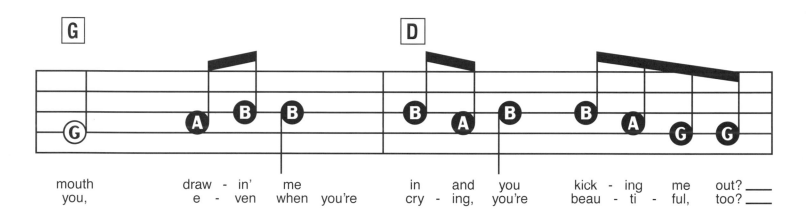

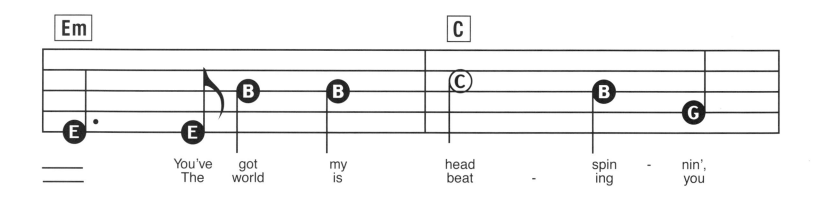

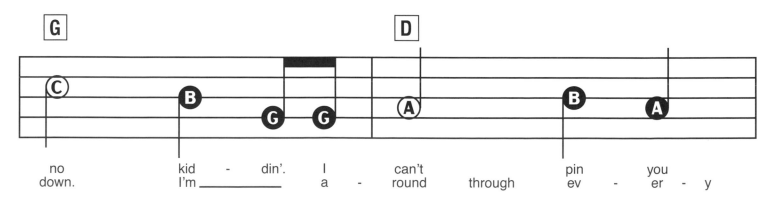

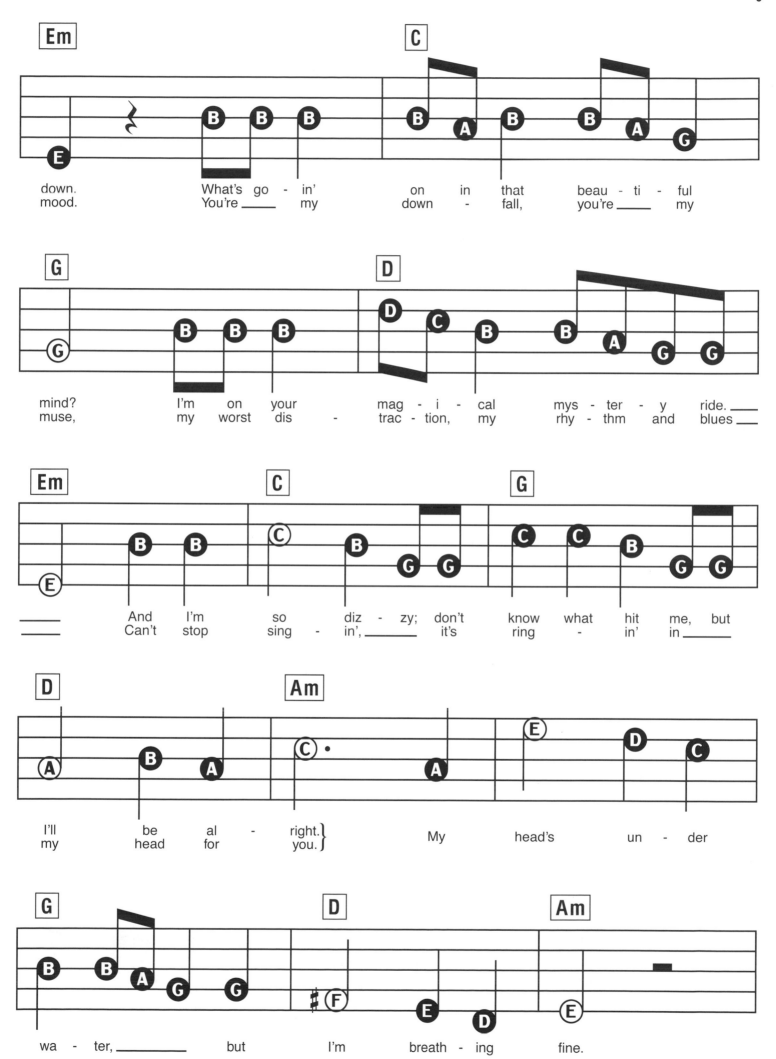

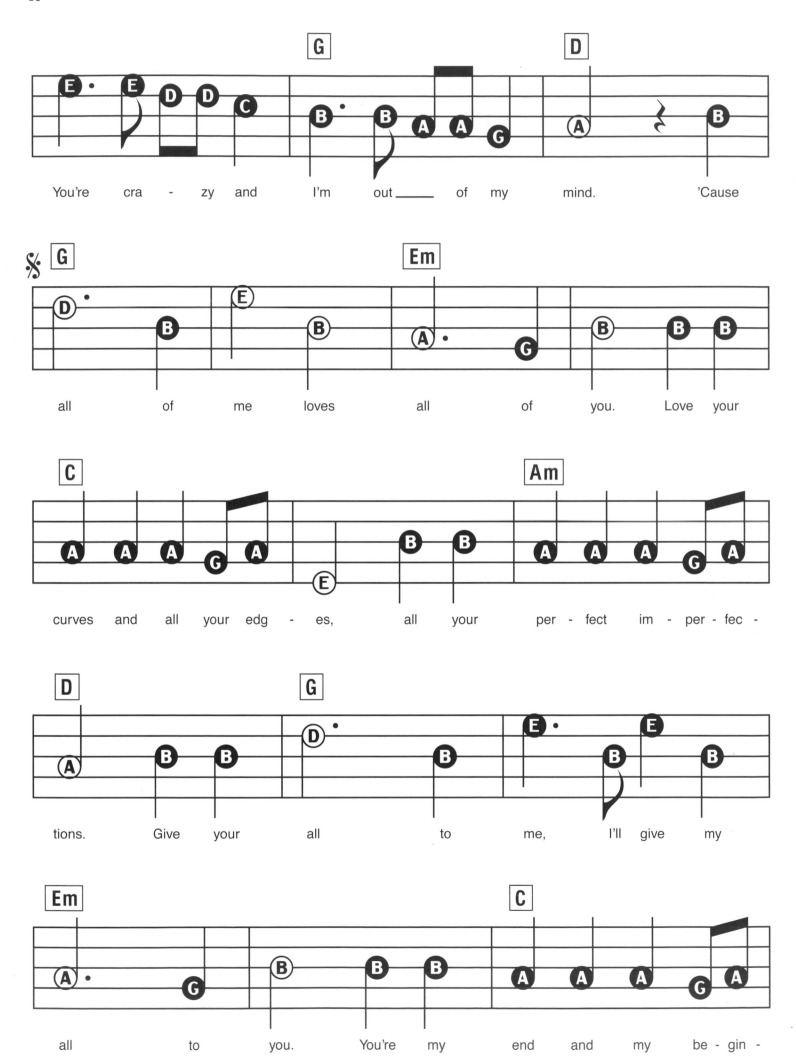

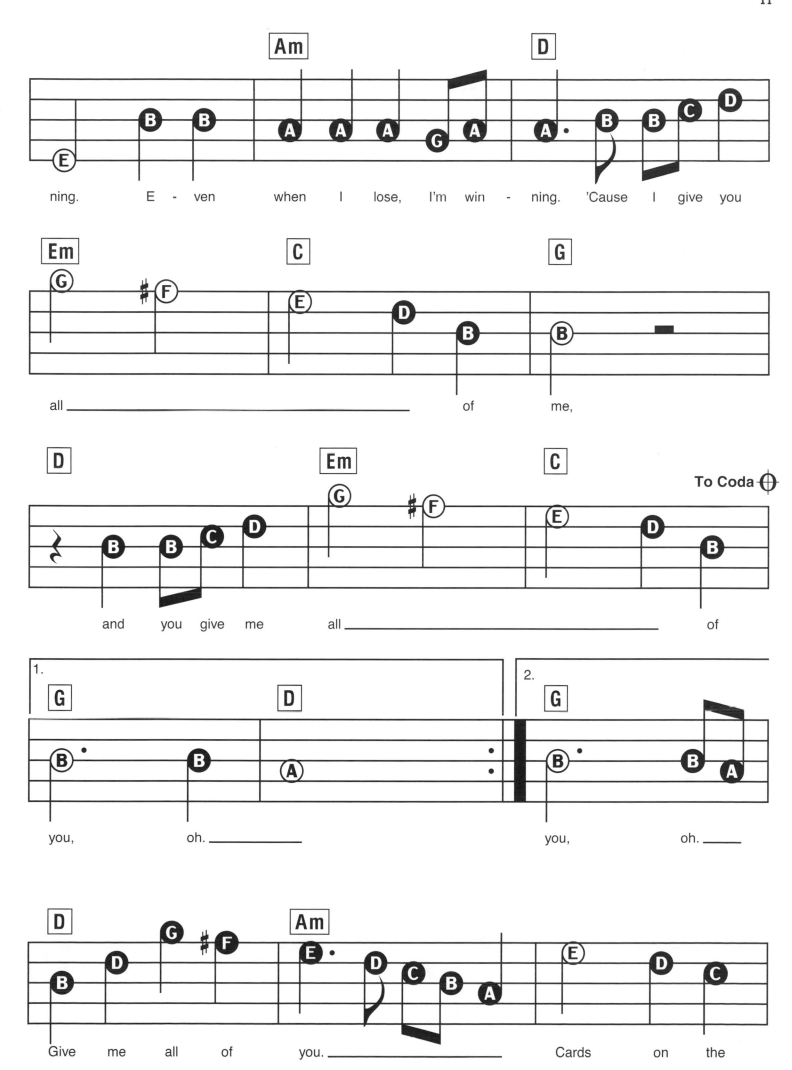

12

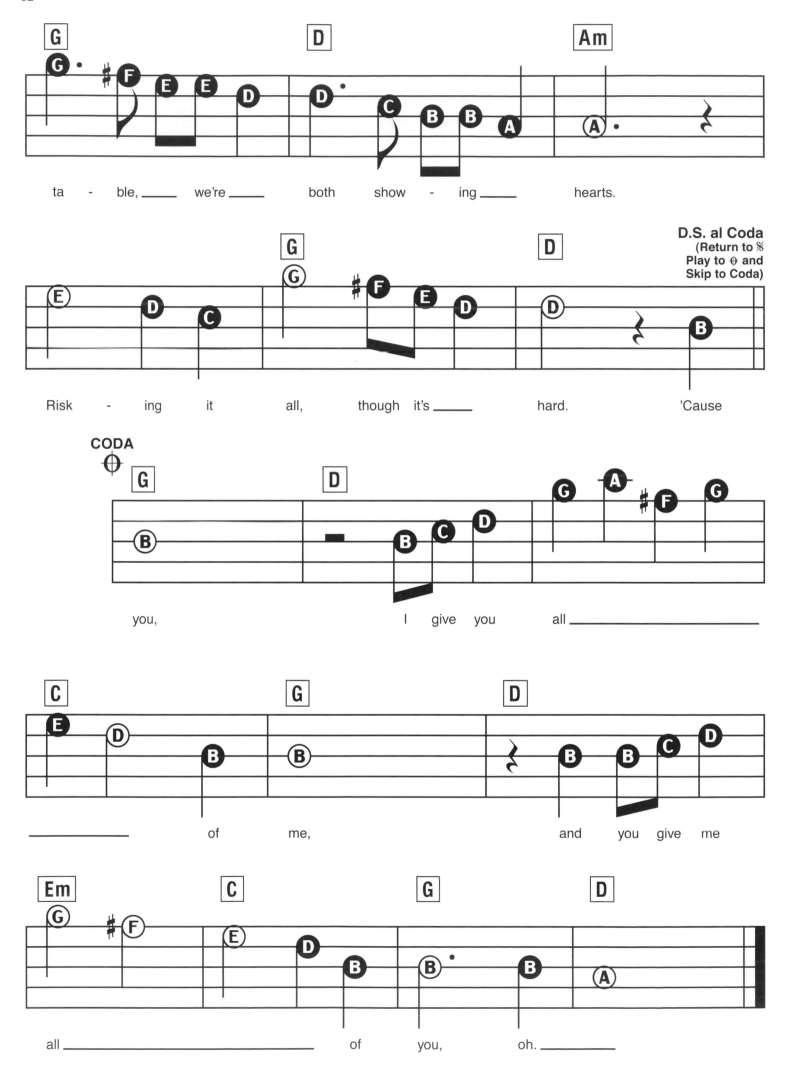

ta - ble, _____ we're _____ both show - ing _____ hearts.

D.S. al Coda
(Return to %
Play to ⊕ and
Skip to Coda)

Risk - ing it all, though it's _____ hard. 'Cause

CODA

you, I give you all _____

_____ of me, and you give me

all _____ of you, oh. _____

Get Lucky

Registration 4
Rhythm: Dance or Rock

Words and Music by Thomas Bangalter,
Guy Manuel Homem Christo,
Pharrell Williams and Nile Rodgers

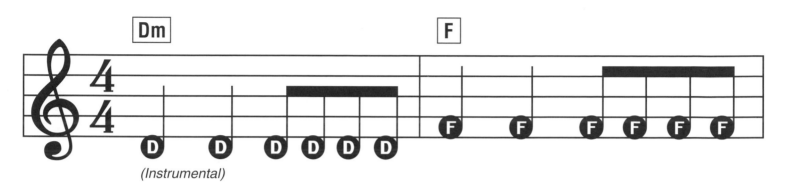

(Instrumental)

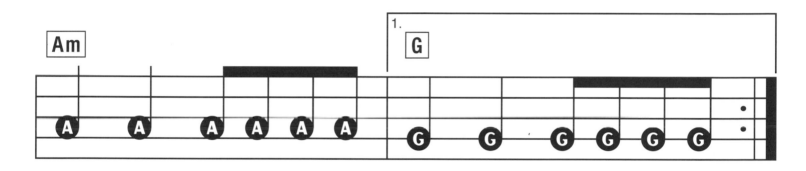

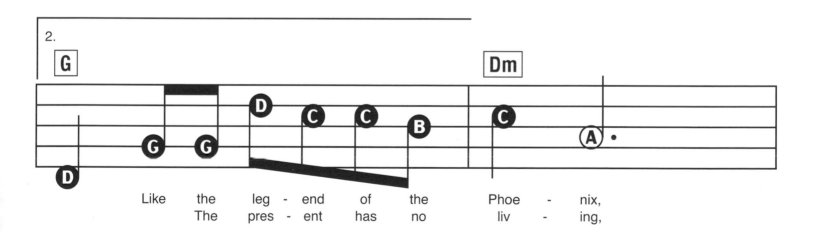

Like   the   leg - end   of   the   Phoe - nix,
The   pres - ent   has   no   liv - ing,

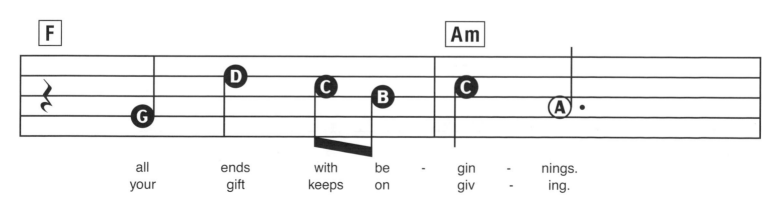

all   ends   with   be - gin - nings.
your   gift   keeps   on   giv - ing.

14

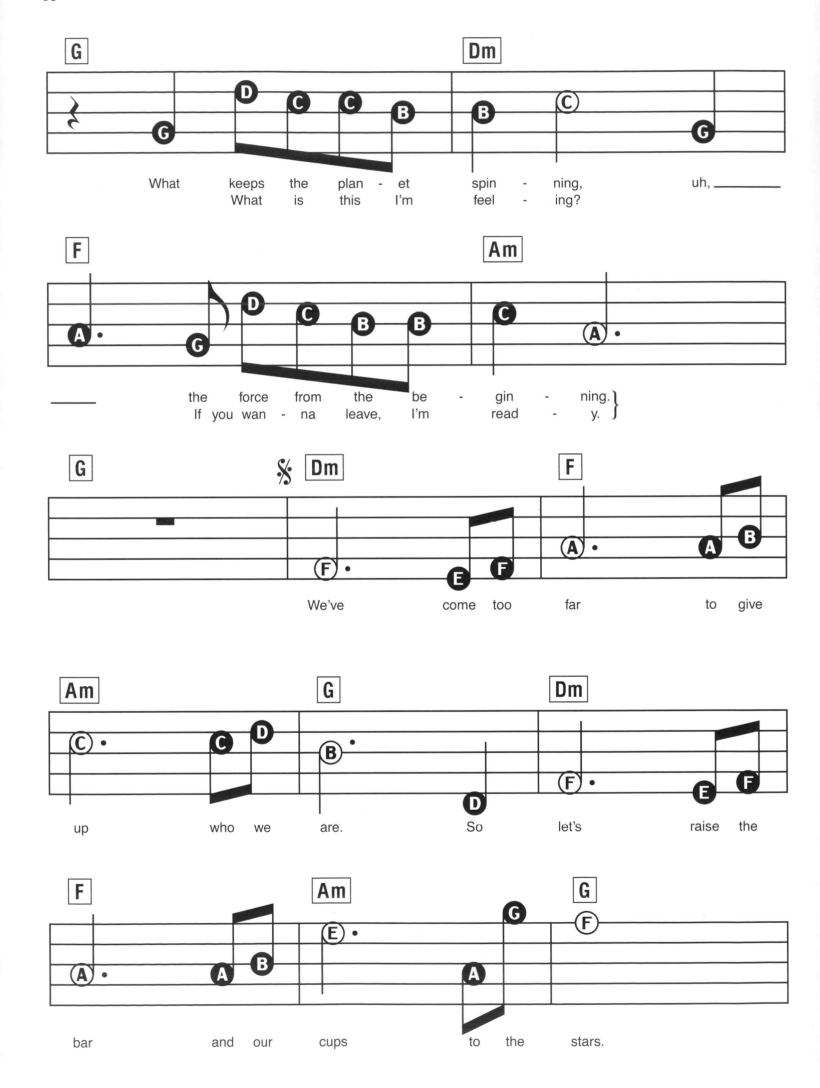

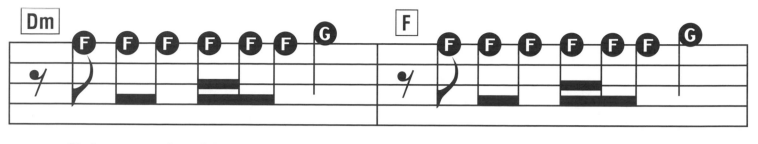

She's up all night 'til the sun.

I'm up all night to get some.

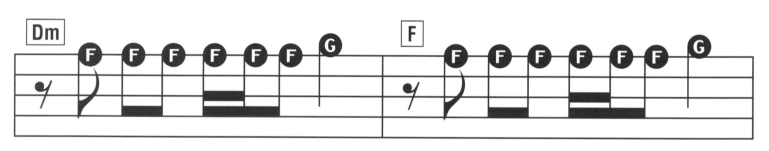

She's up all night for good fun.

I'm up all night to get luck - y.

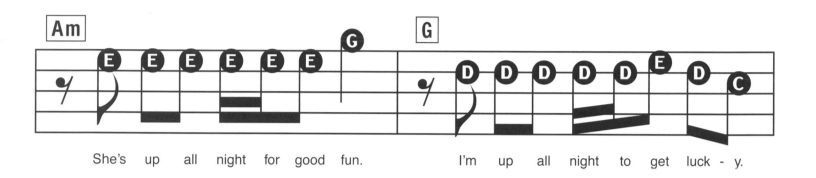

We're up all night 'til the sun.

We're up all night to get some.

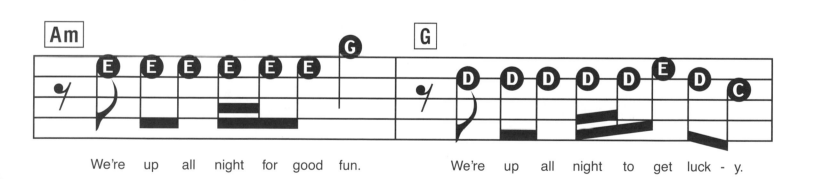

We're up all night for good fun.

We're up all night to get luck - y.

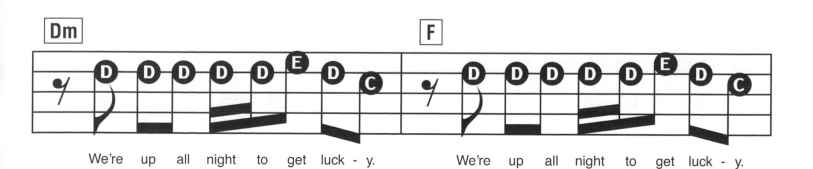

We're up all night to get luck - y.

We're up all night to get luck - y.

16

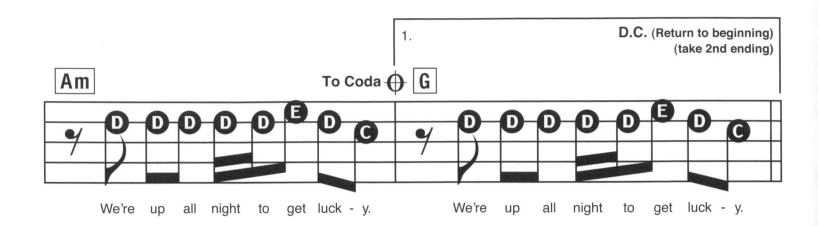

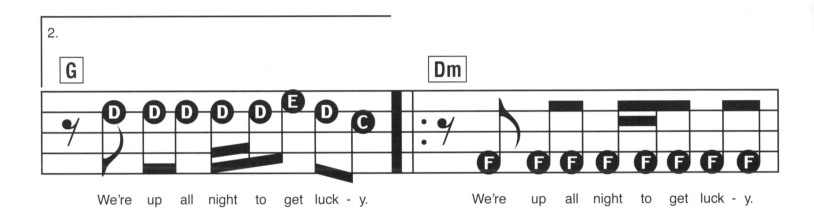

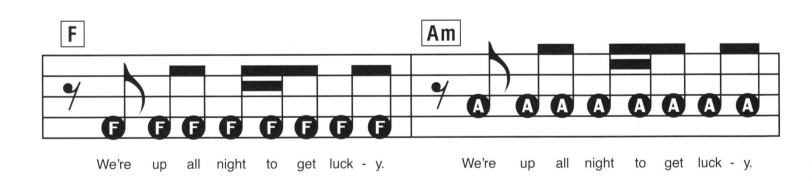

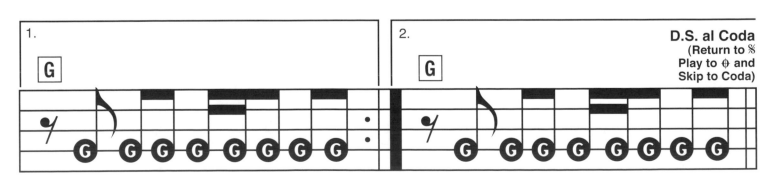

CODA

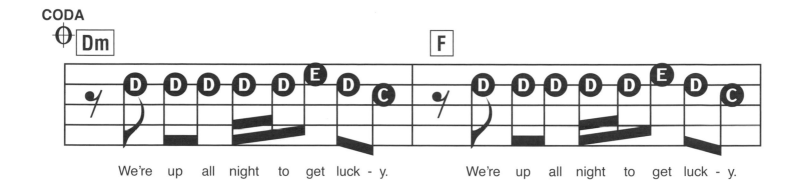

We're up all night to get luck - y.   We're up all night to get luck - y.

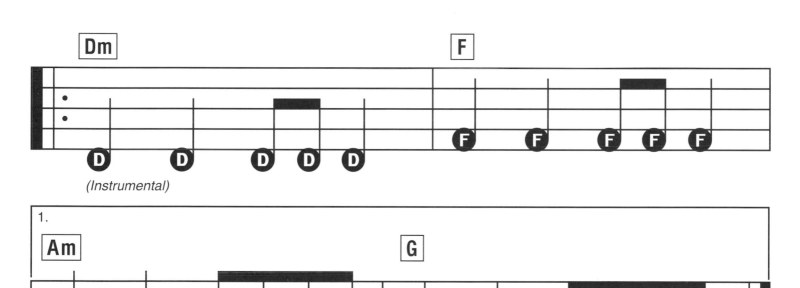

We're up all night to get luck - y.   We're up all night to get luck - y.

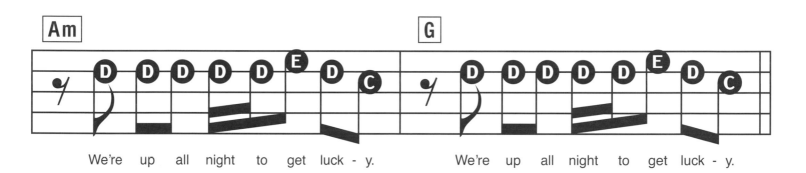

(Instrumental)

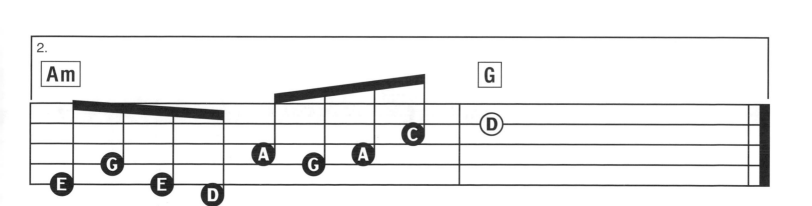

Brave

Registration 2
Rhythm: Pop or Rock

Words and Music by Sara Bareilles
and Jack Antonoff

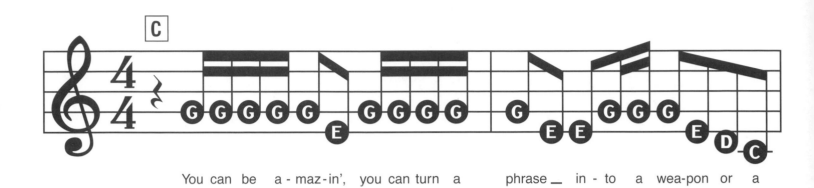

You can be a - maz-in', you can turn a phrase _ in - to a wea-pon or a

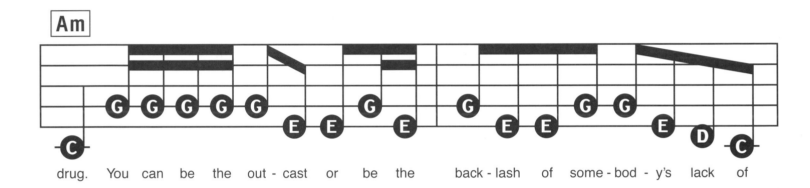

drug. You can be the out - cast or be the back - lash of some - bod - y's lack of

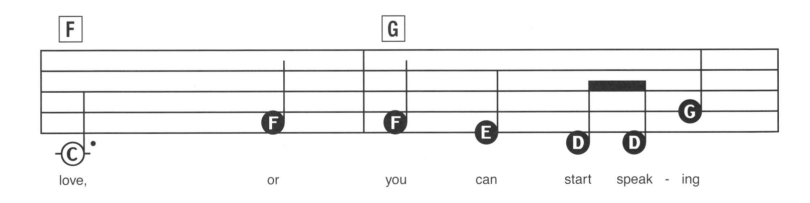

love, or you can start speak - ing

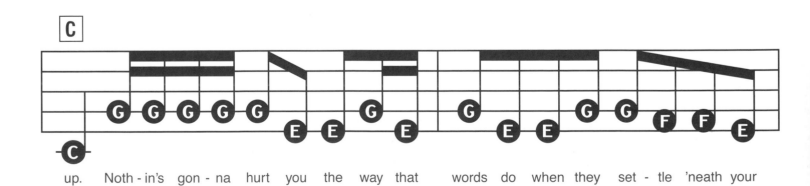

up. Noth - in's gon - na hurt you the way that words do when they set - tle 'neath your

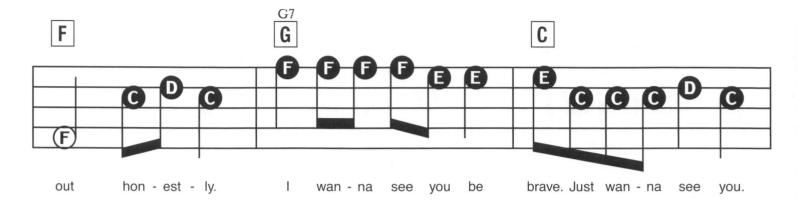

out hon - est - ly. I wan - na see you be brave. Just wan - na see you.

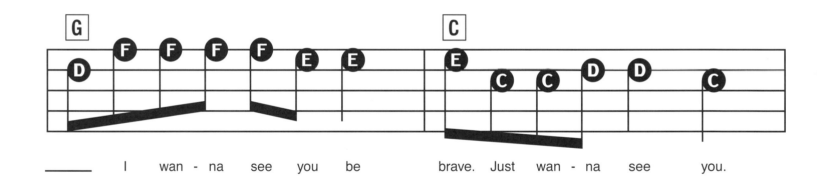

I just wan - na see _____ you. I just wan - na see you. _____

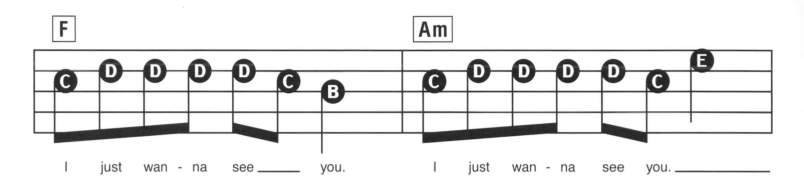

_____ I wan - na see you be brave. Just wan - na see you.

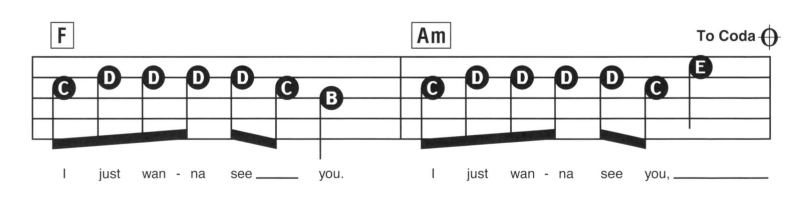

I just wan - na see _____ you. I just wan - na see you, _____

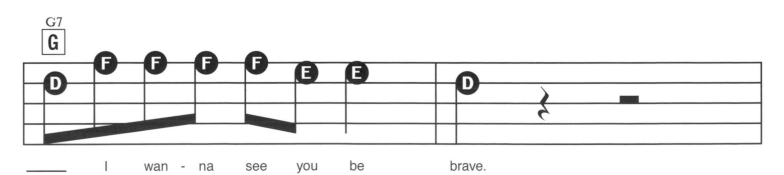

_____ I wan - na see you be brave.

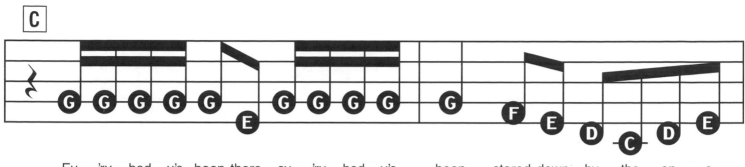

Ev - 'ry - bod - y's been there, ev - 'ry - bod - y's been stared down by the en - e -

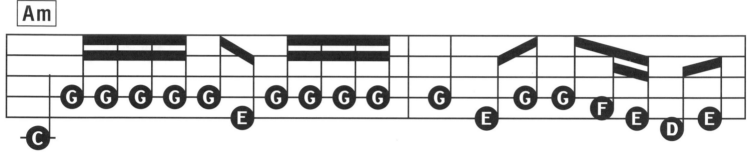

my. Fall - en for the fear and done some dis - ap - pear - in', bow down to the might - y.

Don't run, just stop hold - in' your

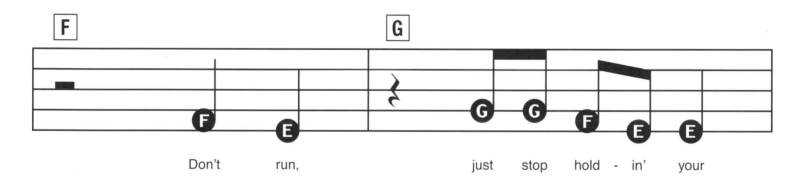

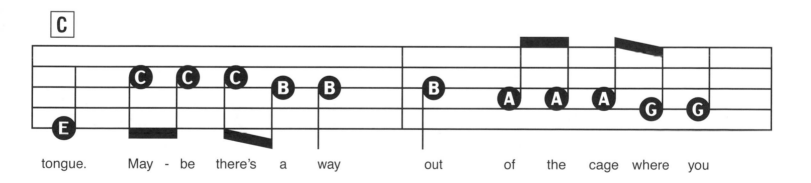

tongue. May - be there's a way out of the cage where you

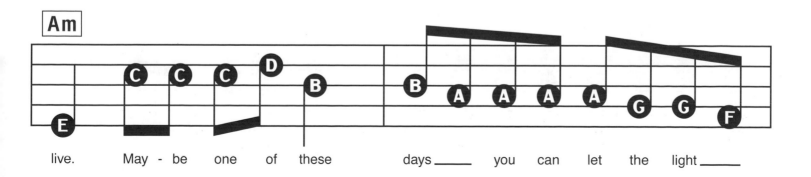

live. May - be one of these days_____ you can let the light_____

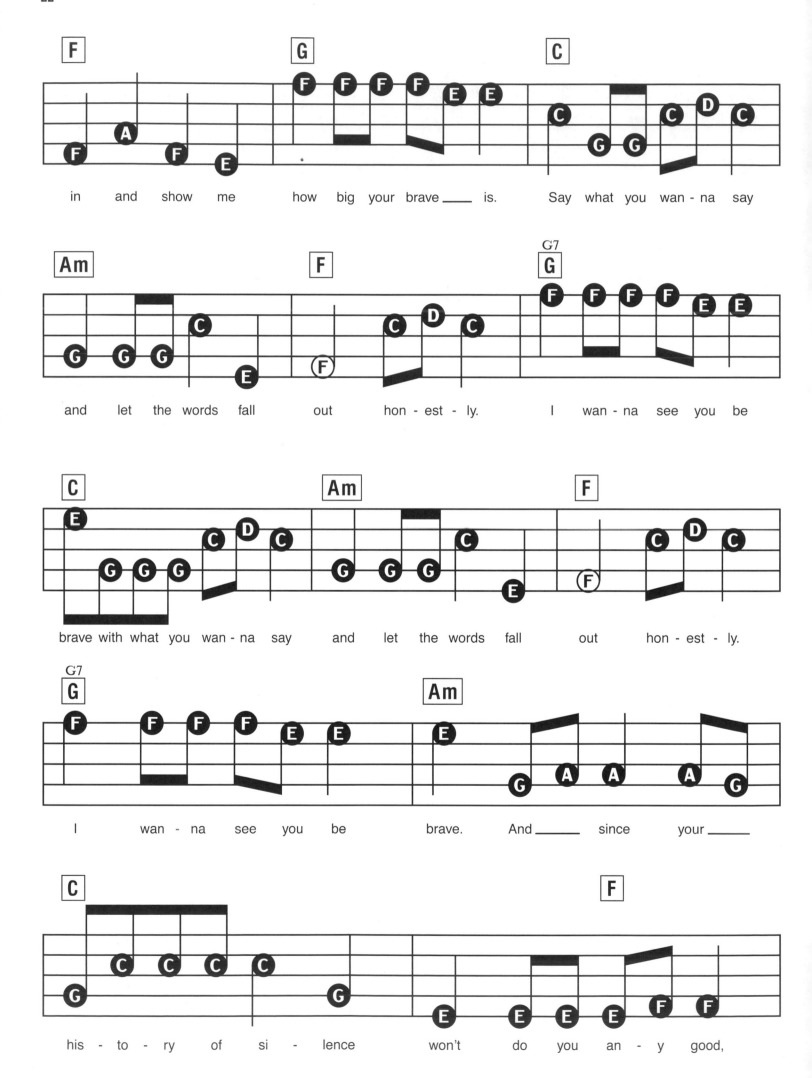

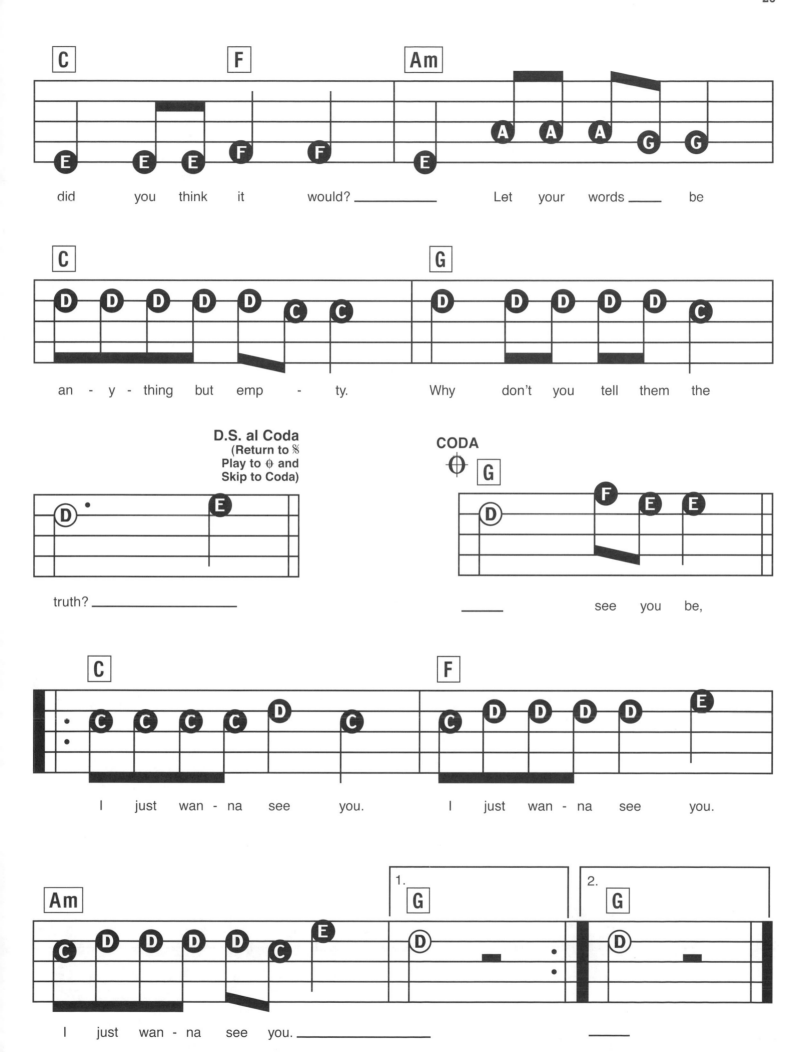

Let Her Go

Registration 4
Rhythm: Folk or Rock

Words and Music by
Michael David Rosenberg

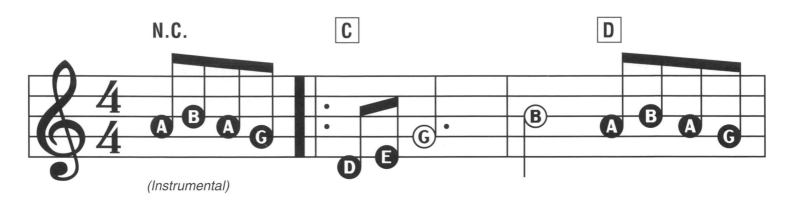

(Instrumental)

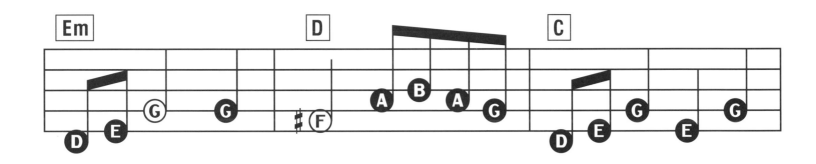

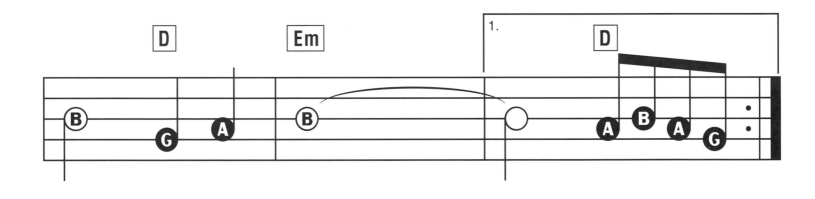

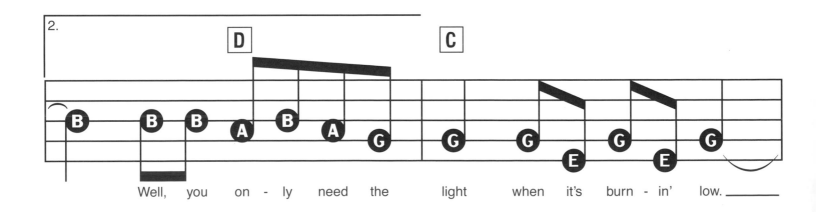

Well, you on-ly need the light when it's burn-in' low. ____

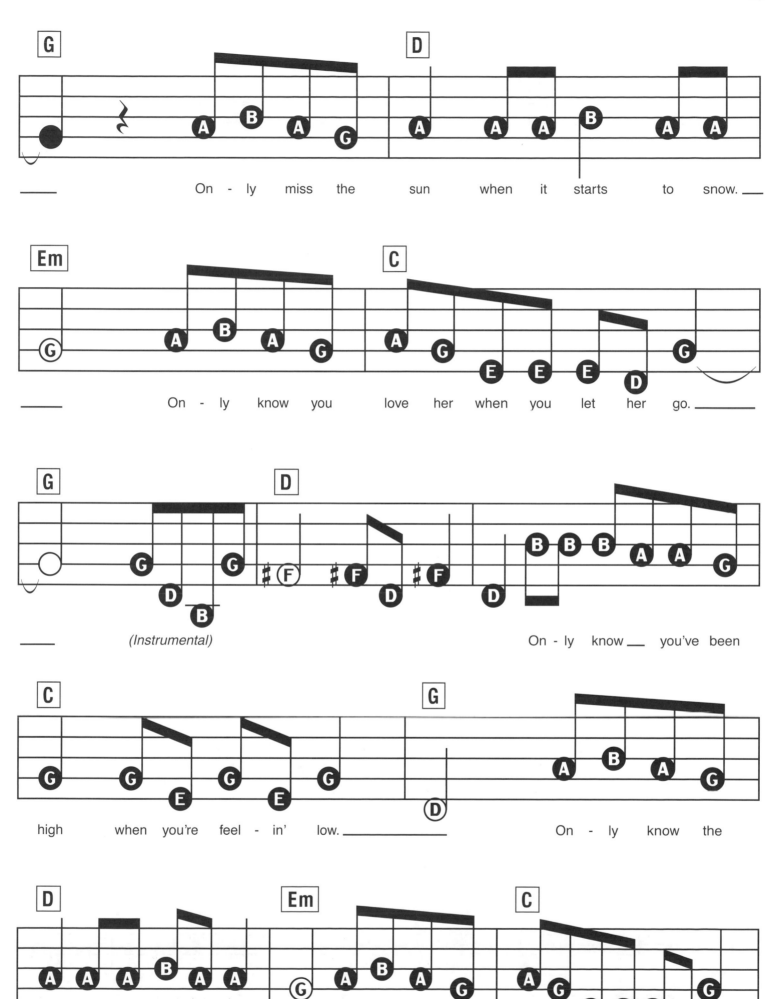

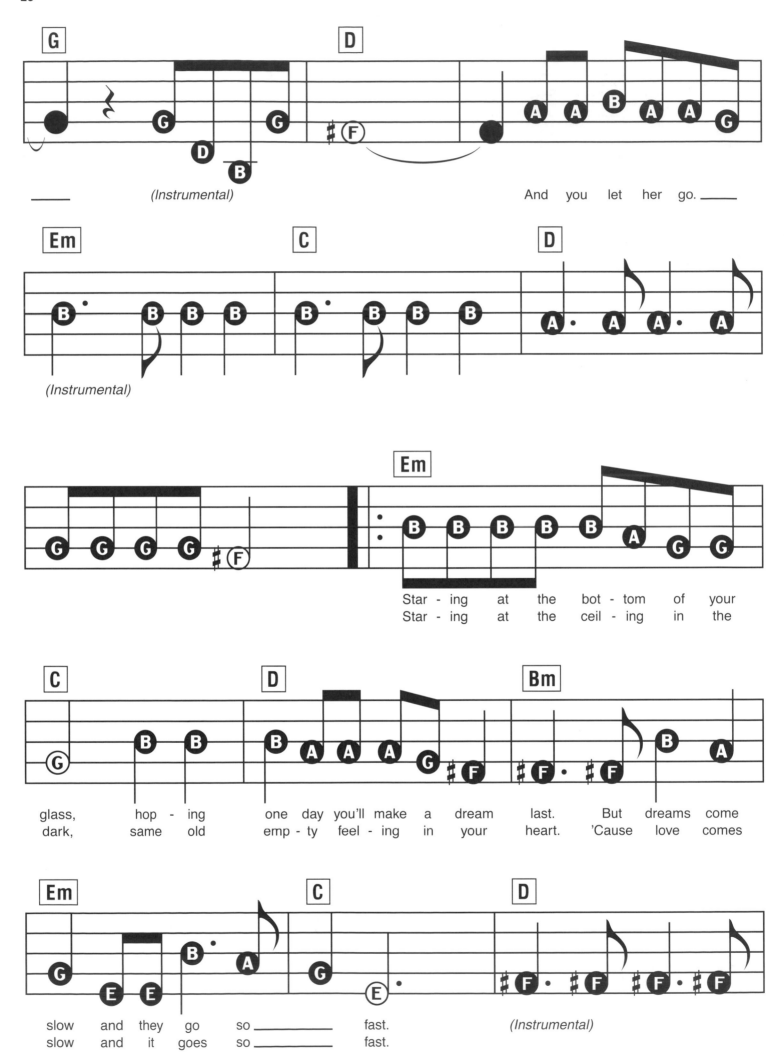

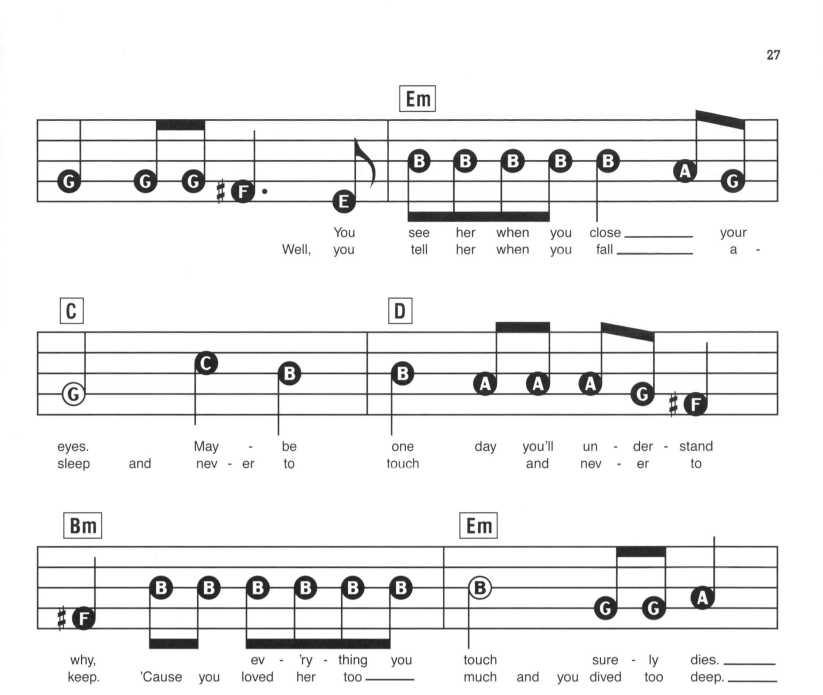

Em

You see her when you close _____ your
Well, you tell her when you fall _____ a-

C   **D**

eyes.   May - be   one   day you'll un - der - stand
sleep and   nev - er to   touch   and nev - er to

Bm   **Em**

why,   ev - 'ry - thing you   touch   sure - ly dies. _____
keep.   'Cause you loved her too _____ much and you dived too deep. _____

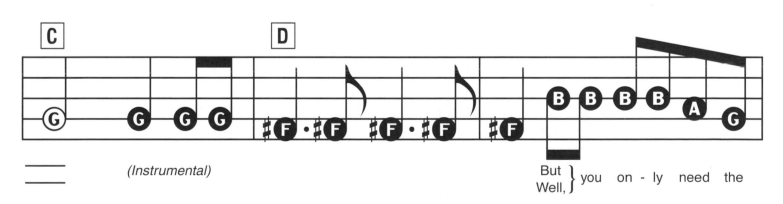

C   **D**

_____   *(Instrumental)*   But ⎱ you on - ly need the
                                                  Well, ⎰

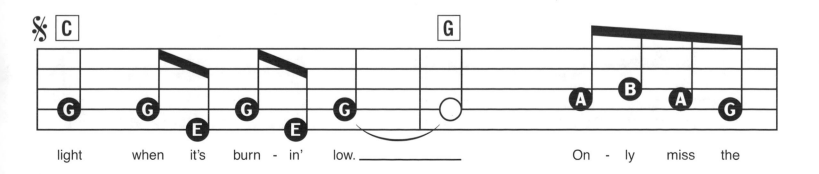

𝄋 **C**   **G**

light   when it's burn - in' low. _____   On - ly miss the

28

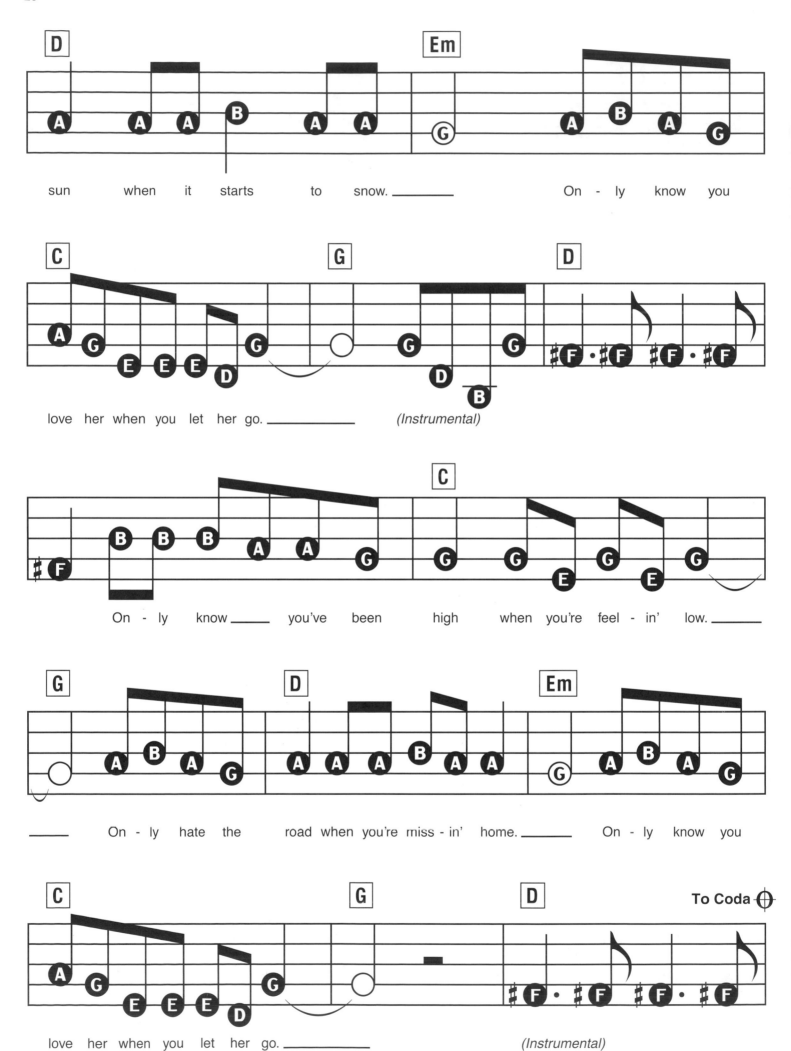

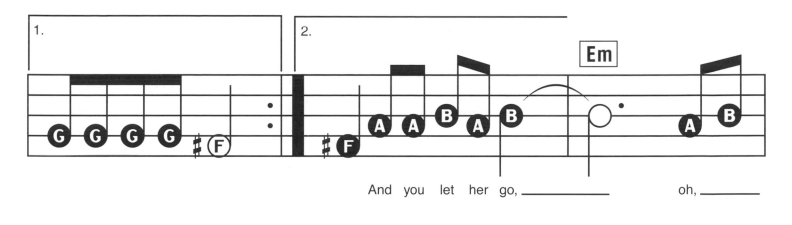

And you let her go, _____ oh, _____

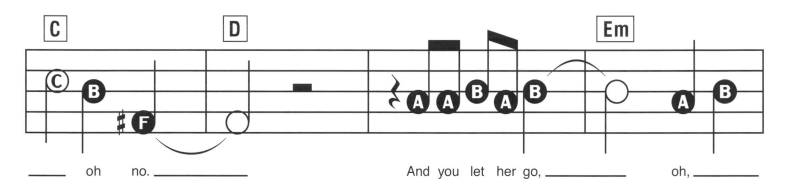

_____ oh no. _____ And you let her go, _____ oh, _____

D.S. al Coda
(Return to 𝄋
Play to ⊕ and
Skip to Coda)

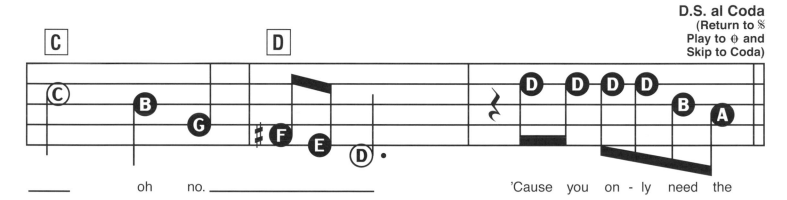

_____ oh no. _____ 'Cause you on - ly need the

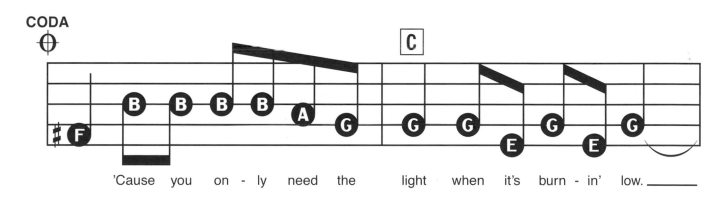

CODA

'Cause you on - ly need the light when it's burn - in' low. _____

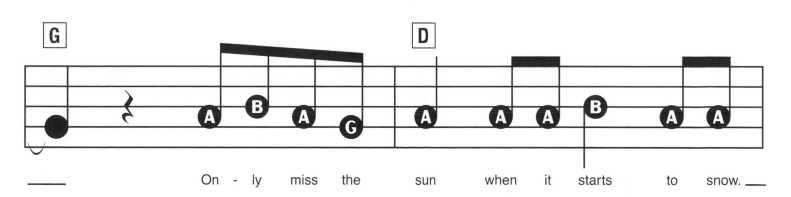

On - ly miss the sun when it starts to snow. __

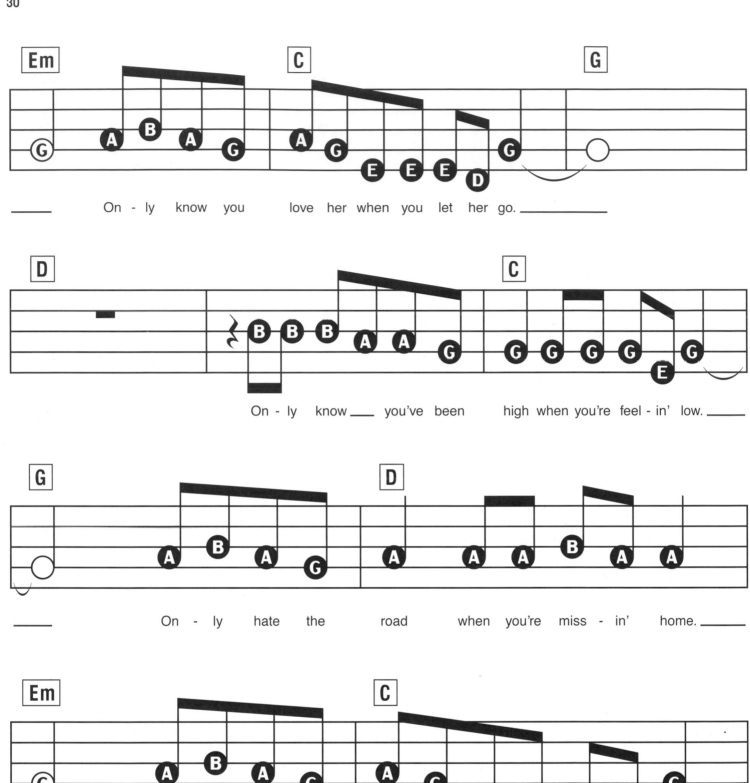

On - ly know you love her when you let her go. ____

On - ly know ____ you've been high when you're feel - in' low. ____

On - ly hate the road when you're miss - in' home. ____

On - ly know you love her when you let her go. ____

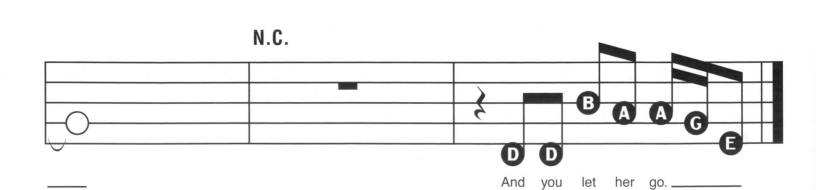

And you let her go. ____

Happy

from DESPICABLE ME 2

Registration 8
Rhythm: Rock

Words and Music by
Pharrell Williams

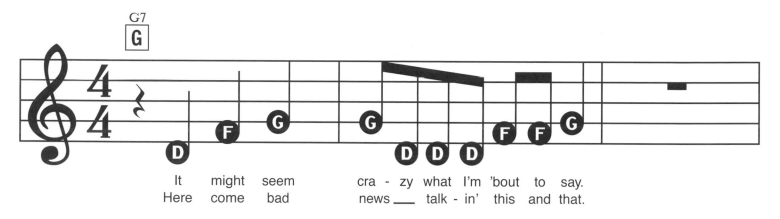

It might seem cra - zy what I'm 'bout to say.
Here come bad news ___ talk - in' this and that.

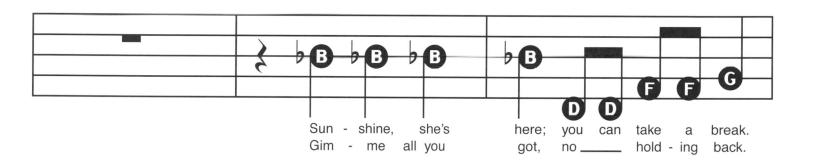

Sun - shine, she's here; you can take a break.
Gim - me all you got, no ___ hold - ing back.

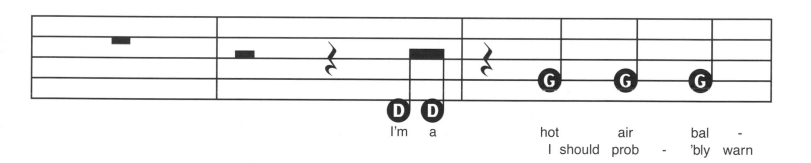

I'm a hot air bal -
I should prob - 'bly warn

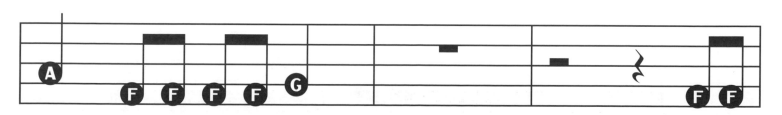

loon that could go to space with the
you, I'll be just ___ fine.

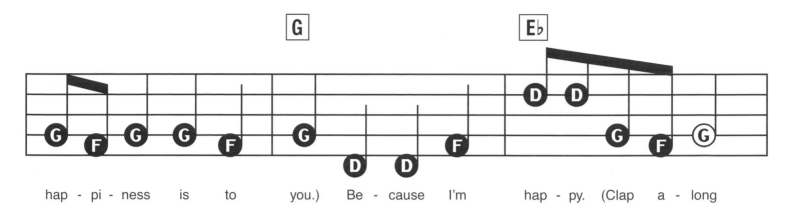

hap - pi - ness is to you.) Be - cause I'm hap - py. (Clap a - long

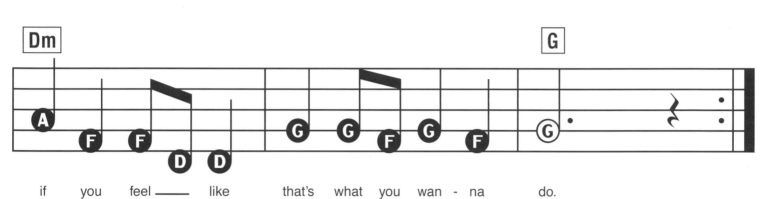

if you feel ____ like that's what you wan - na do.

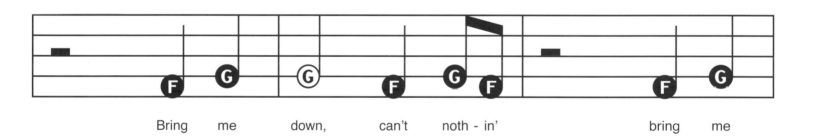

Bring me down, can't noth - in' bring me

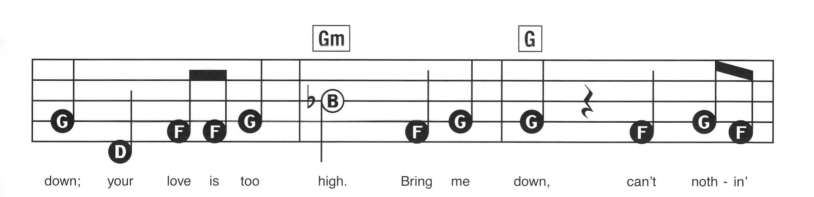

down; your love is too high. Bring me down, can't noth - in'

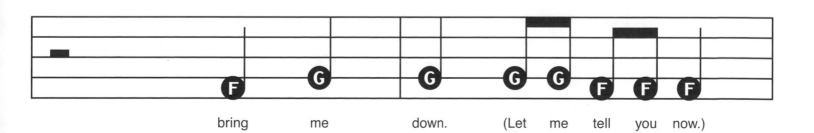

bring me down. (Let me tell you now.)

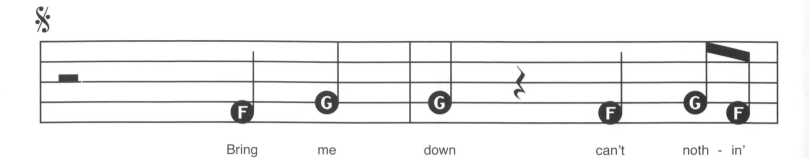

Bring   me   down   can't   noth - in'

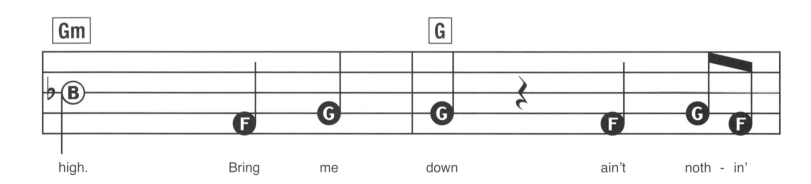

bring   me   down;   your   love   is   too

Gm   **G**

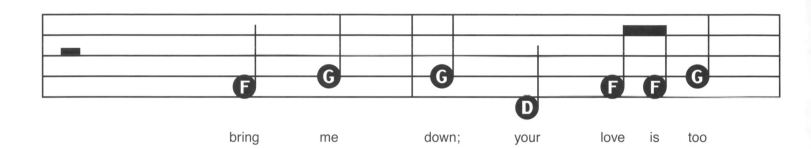

high.   Bring   me   down   ain't   noth - in'

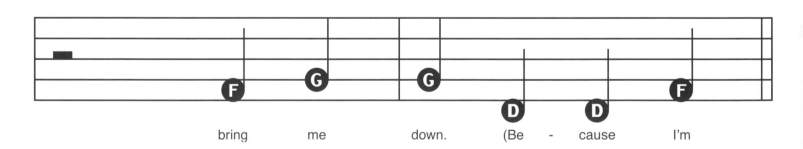

bring   me   down.   (Be   -   cause   I'm

E♭   **Dm**

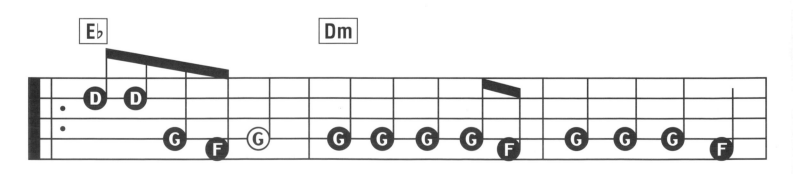

hap - py. (Clap a - long   if   you   feel   like   a   room   with - out   a

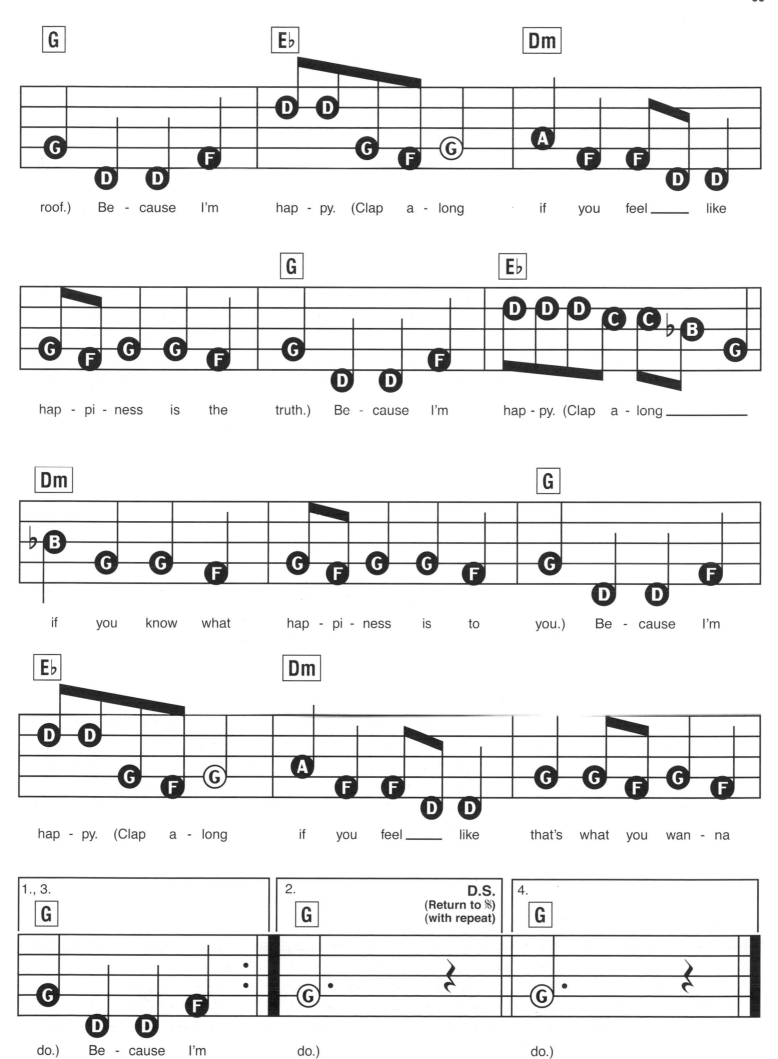

I Won't Give Up

Registration 4
Rhythm: 6/8 March

Words and Music by Jason Mraz
and Michael Natter

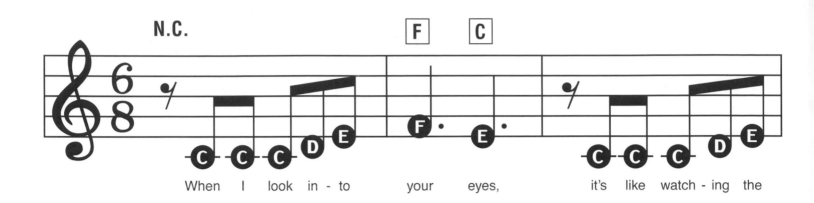

When I look in-to your eyes, it's like watch-ing the

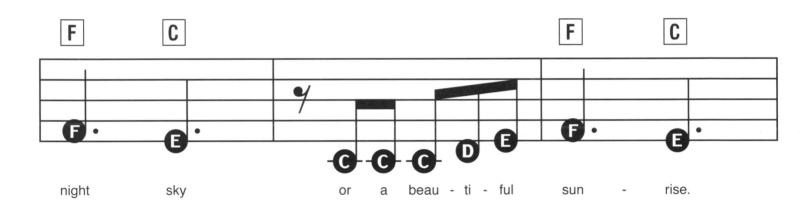

night sky or a beau-ti-ful sun - rise.

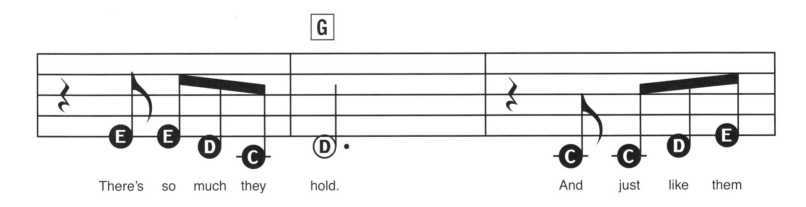

There's so much they hold. And just like them

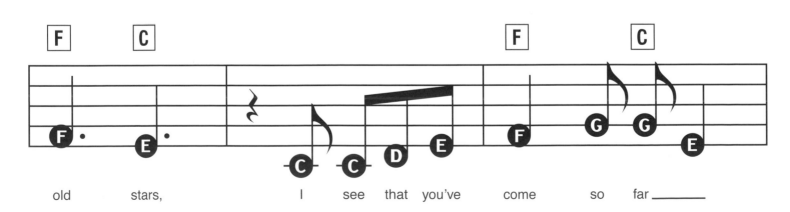

old stars, I see that you've come so far _____

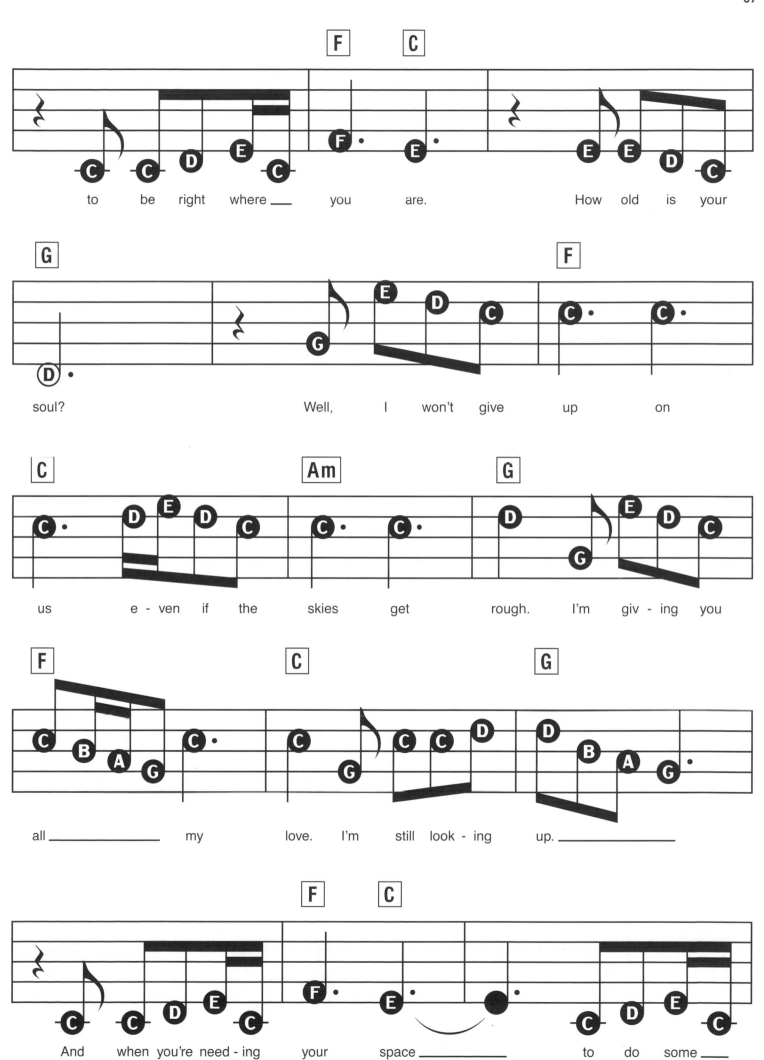

38

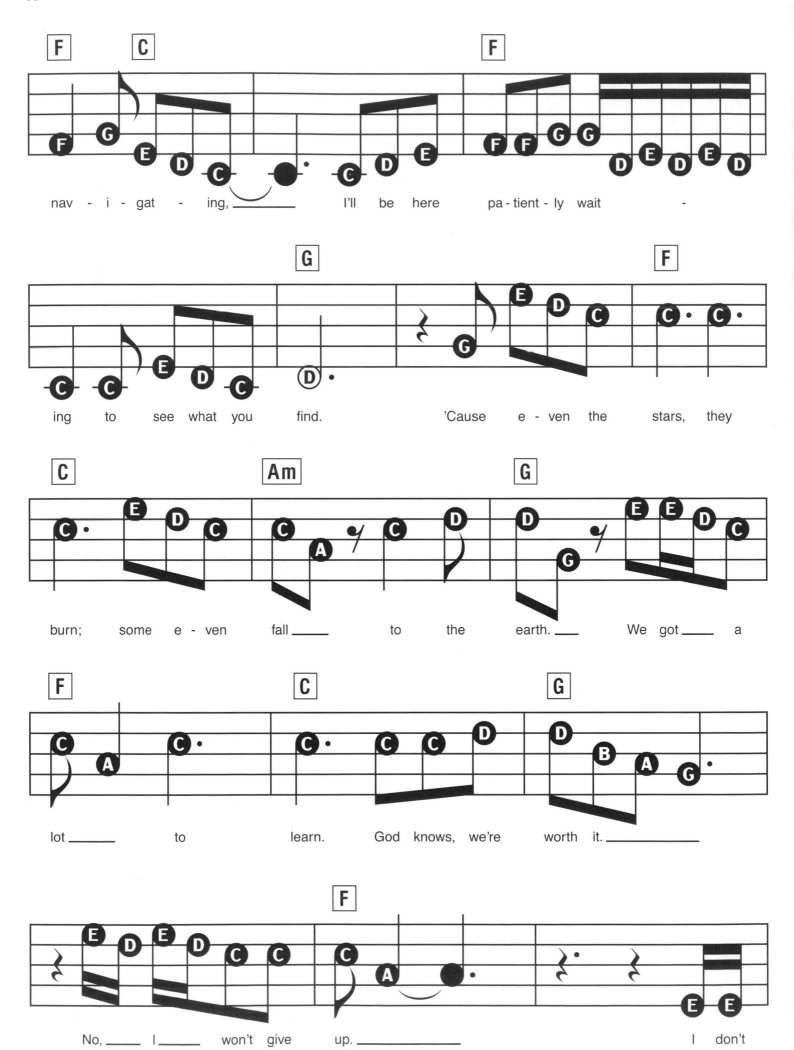

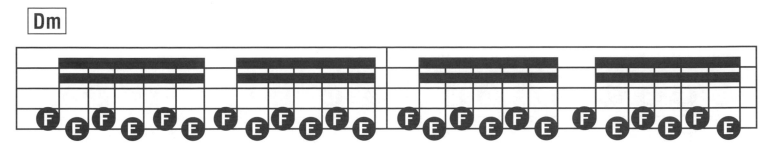

Dm

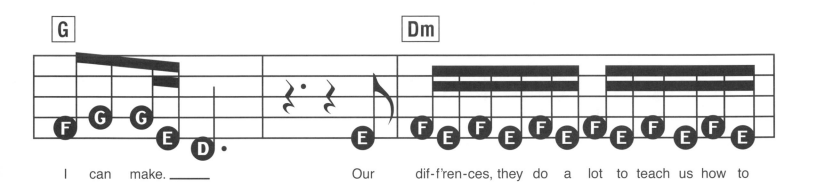

wan-na be some-one who walks a-way so eas-i - ly. I'm here to stay and make the dif - fer-ence that

G   **Dm**

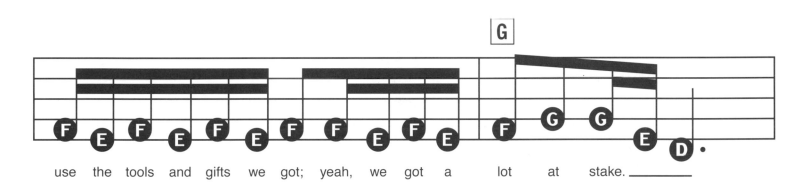

I can make. _____ Our dif-f'ren-ces, they do a lot to teach us how to

G

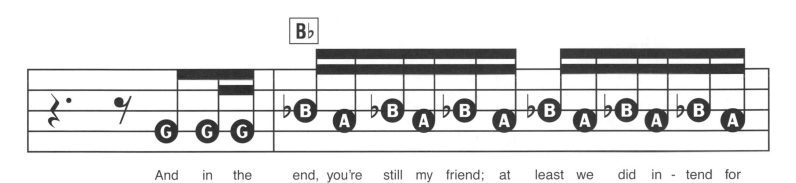

use the tools and gifts we got; yeah, we got a lot at stake. _____

B♭

And in the end, you're still my friend; at least we did in - tend for

G

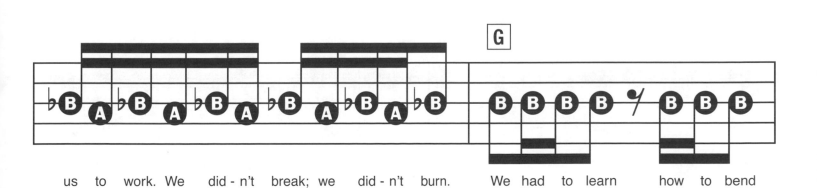

us to work. We did-n't break; we did-n't burn. We had to learn how to bend

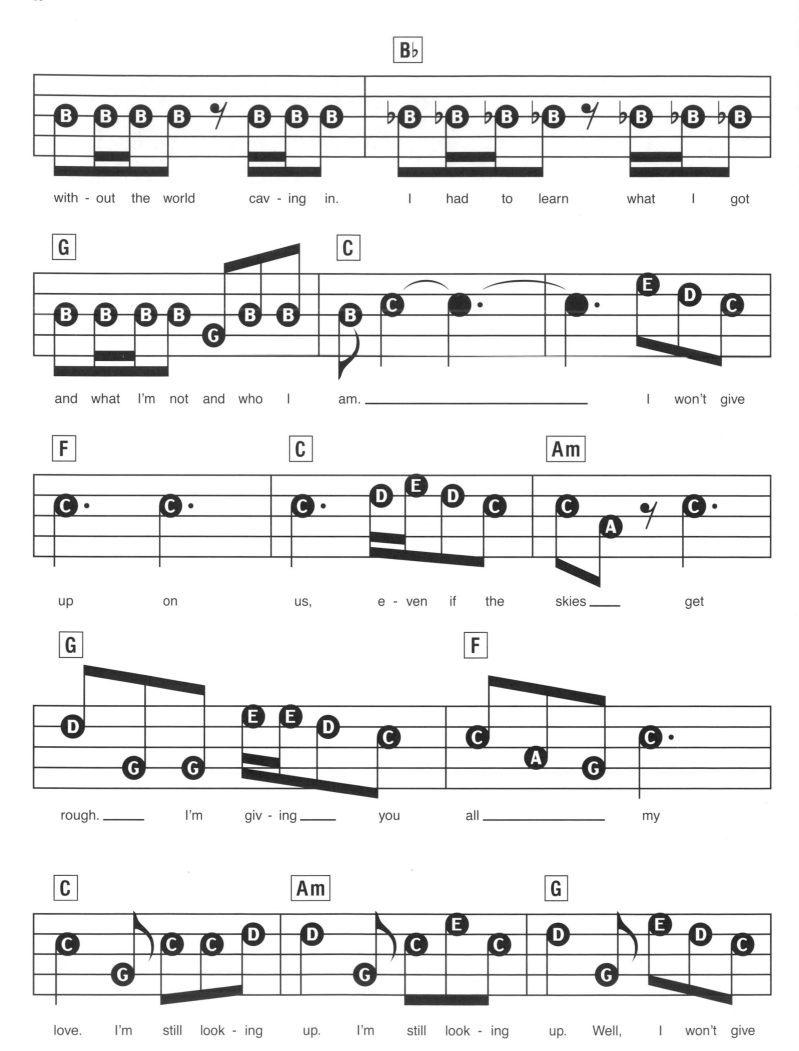

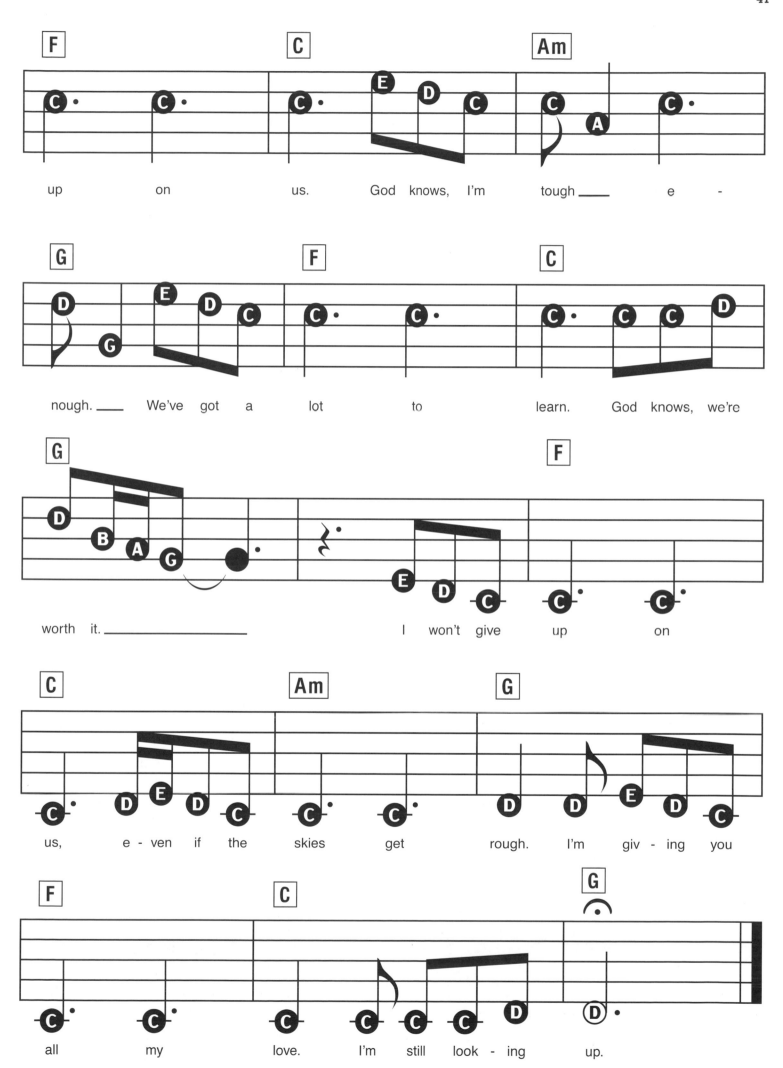

Just Give Me a Reason

Registration 8
Rhythm: 8-Beat or Rock

Words and Music by Alecia Moore,
Jeff Bhasker and Nate Ruess

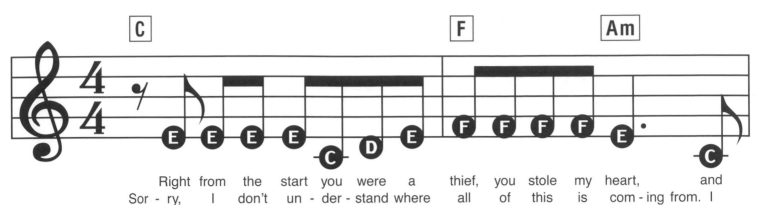

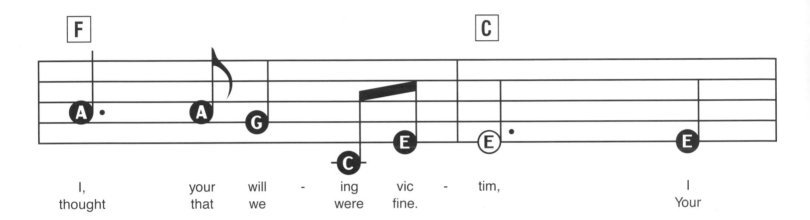

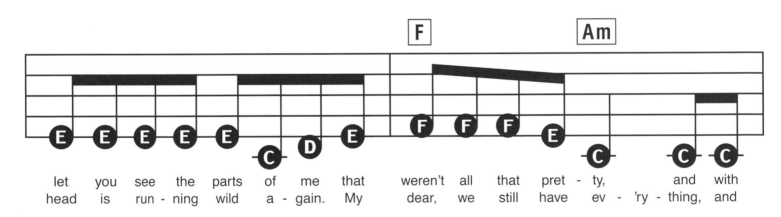

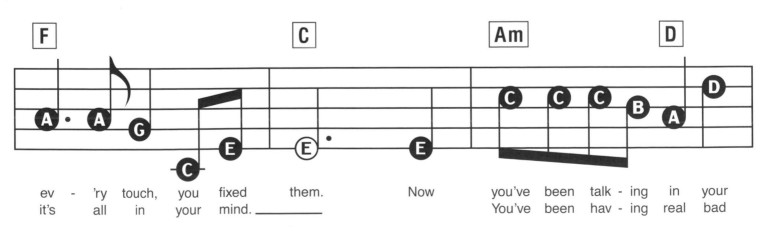

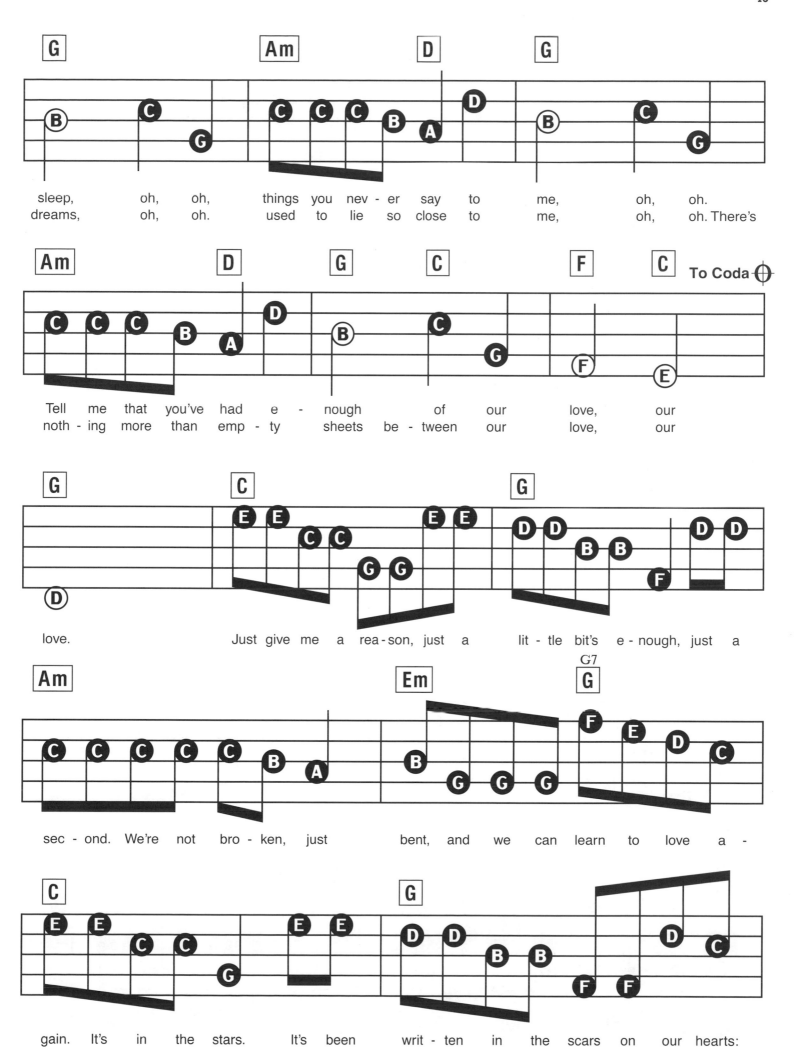

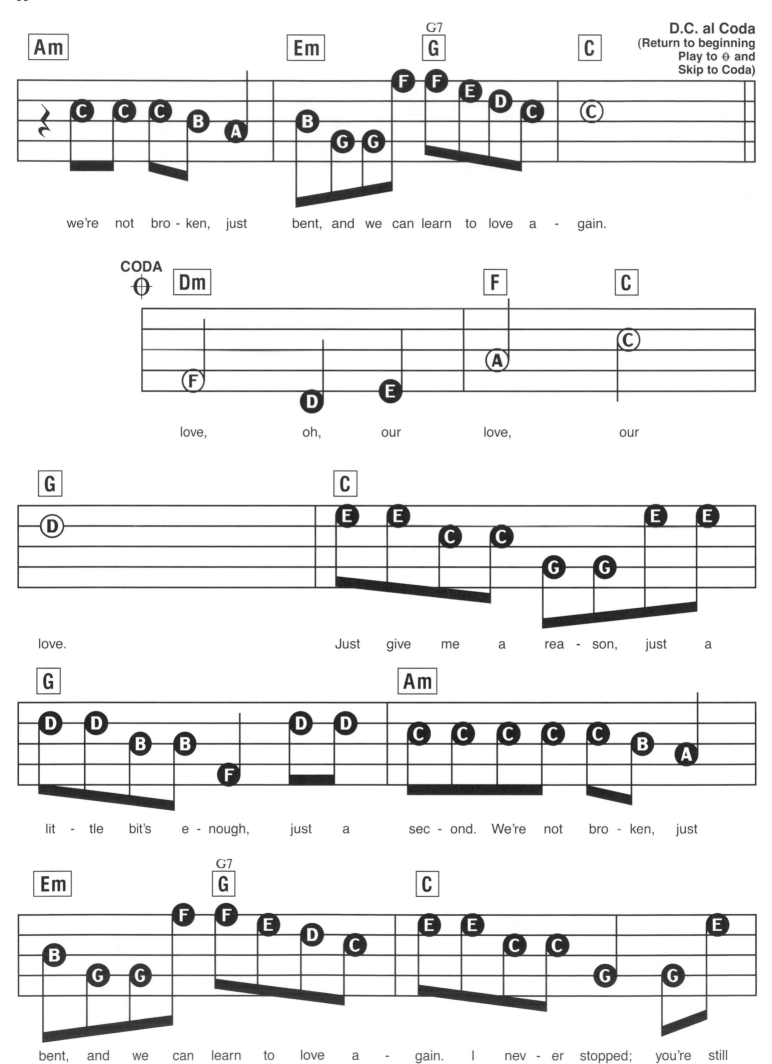

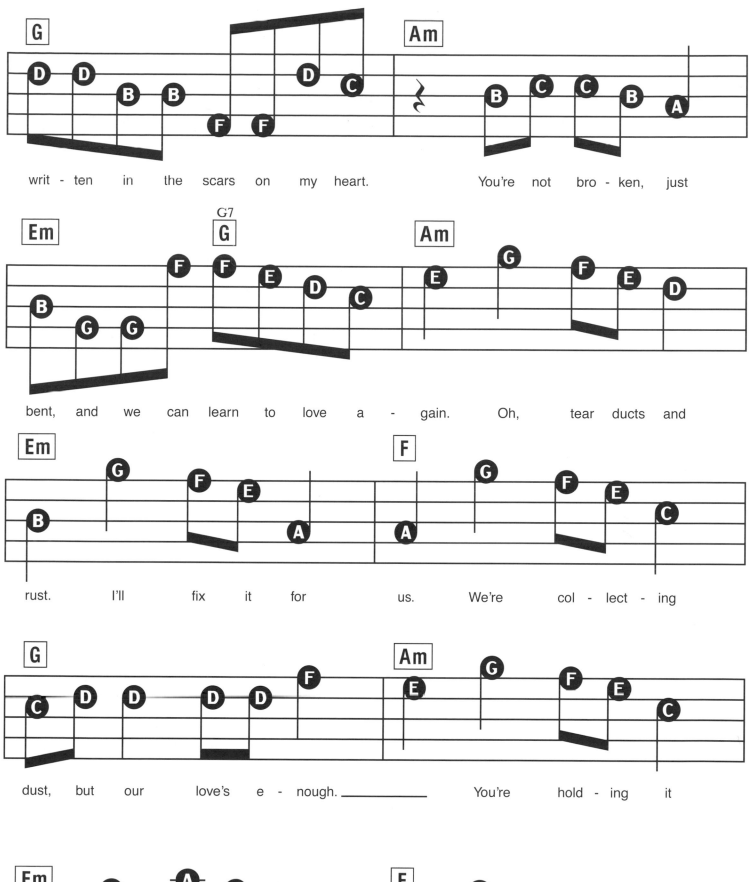

writ - ten in the scars on my heart. You're not bro - ken, just

bent, and we can learn to love a - gain. Oh, tear ducts and

rust. I'll fix it for us. We're col - lect - ing

dust, but our love's e - nough. _____ You're hold - ing it

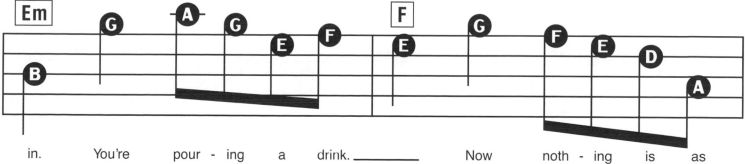

in. You're pour - ing a drink. _____ Now noth - ing is as

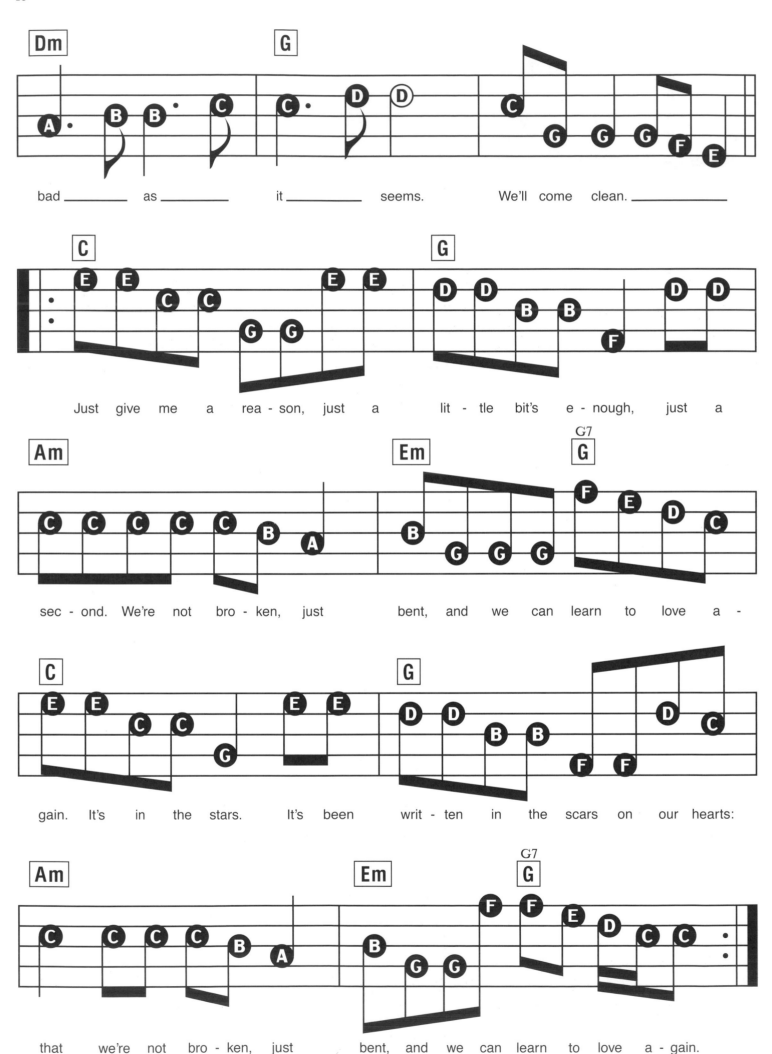

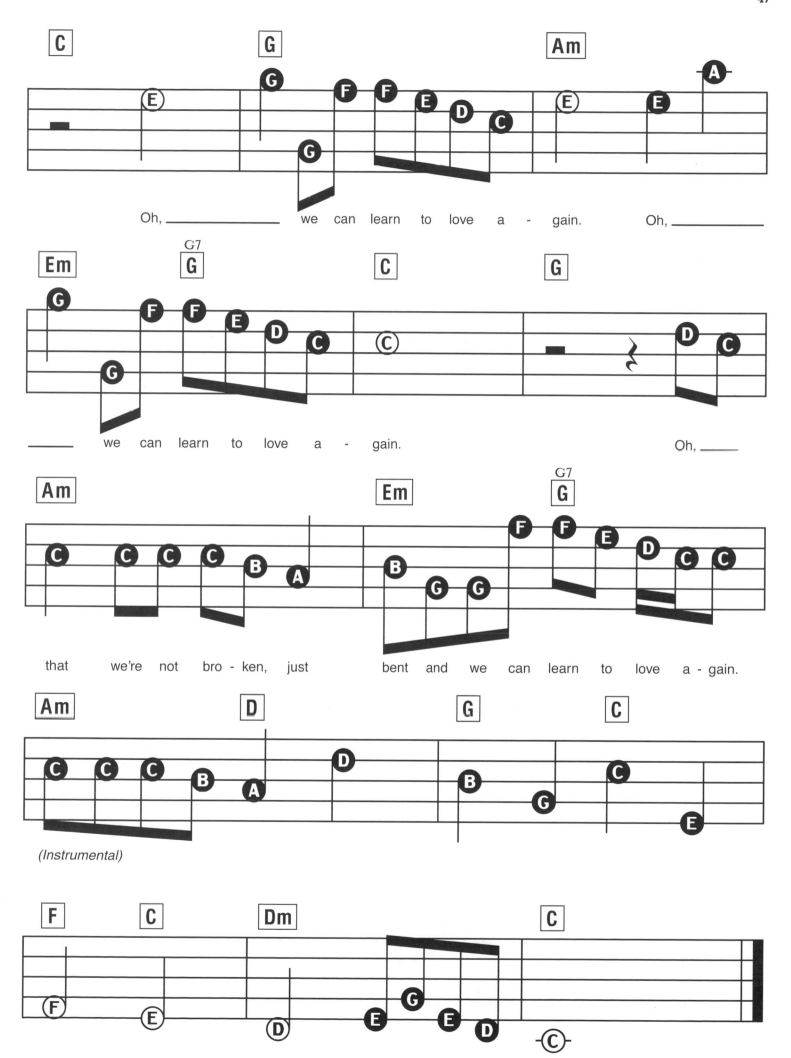

Let It Go
from Disney's Animated Feature FROZEN

Registration 8
Rhythm: Rock or Dance

Music and Lyrics by Kristen Anderson-Lopez
and Robert Lopez

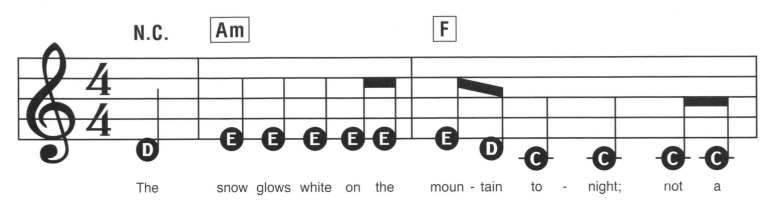

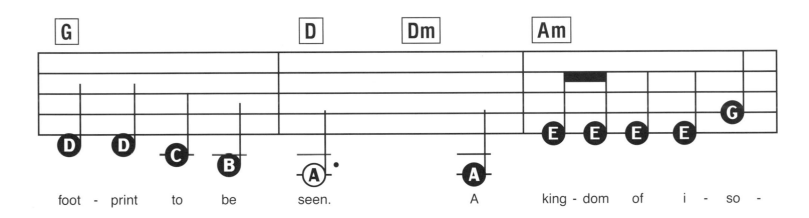

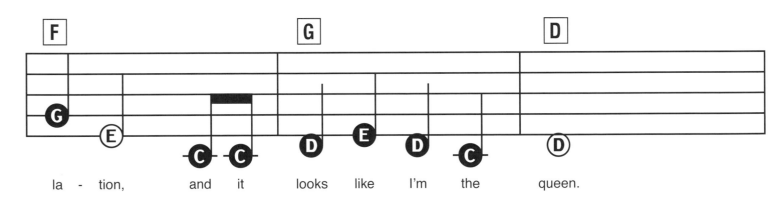

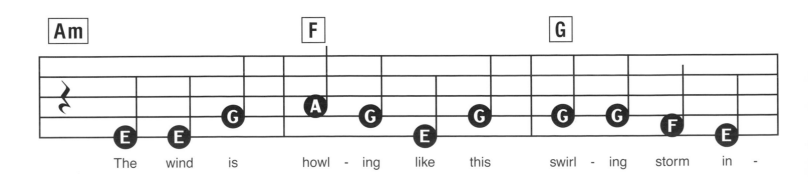

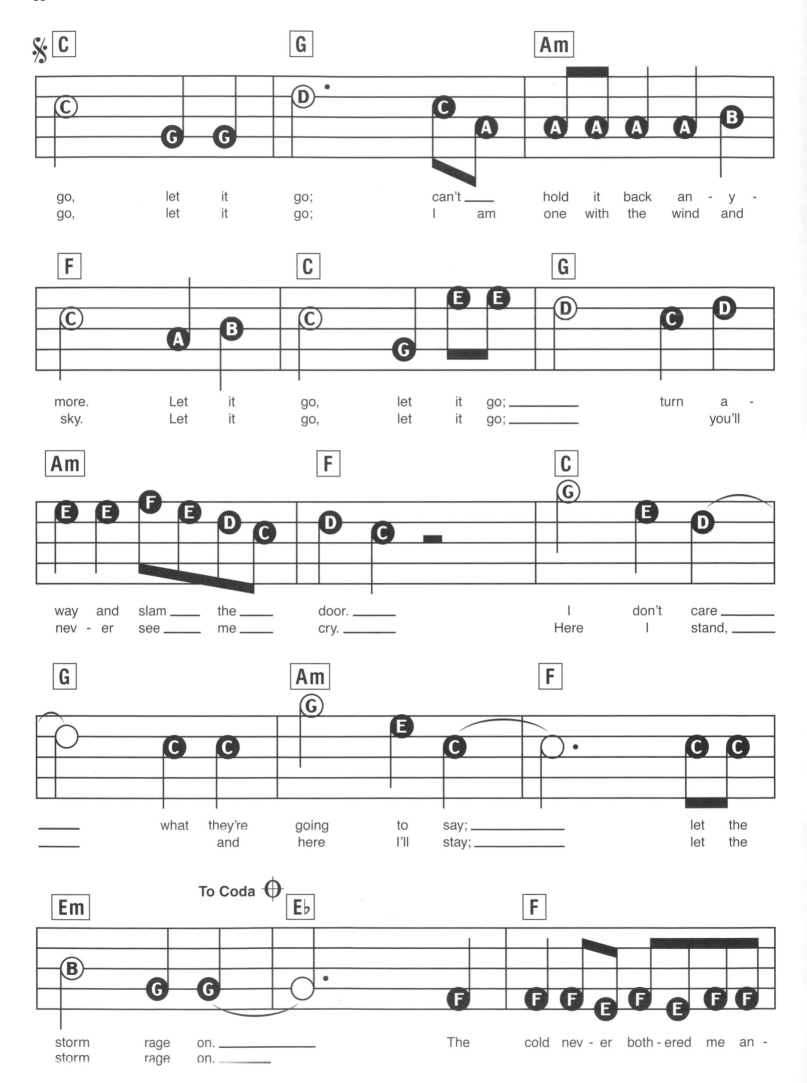

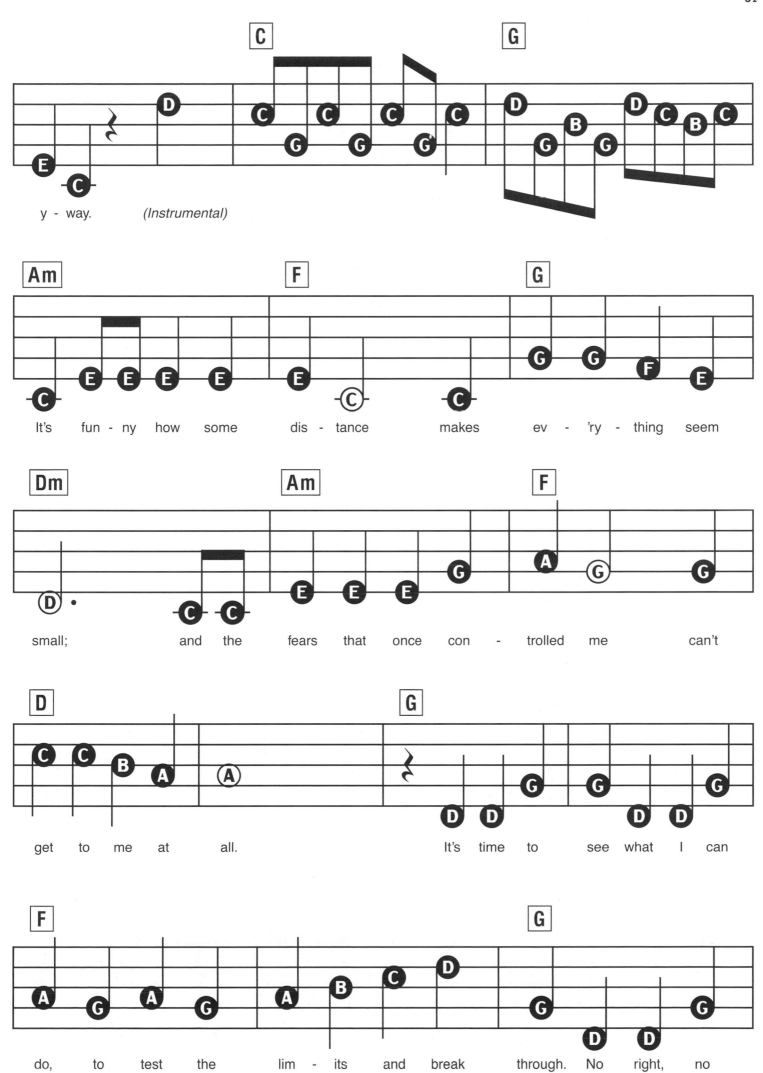

D.S. al Coda
(Return to ℅
Play to ⊕ and
Skip to Coda)

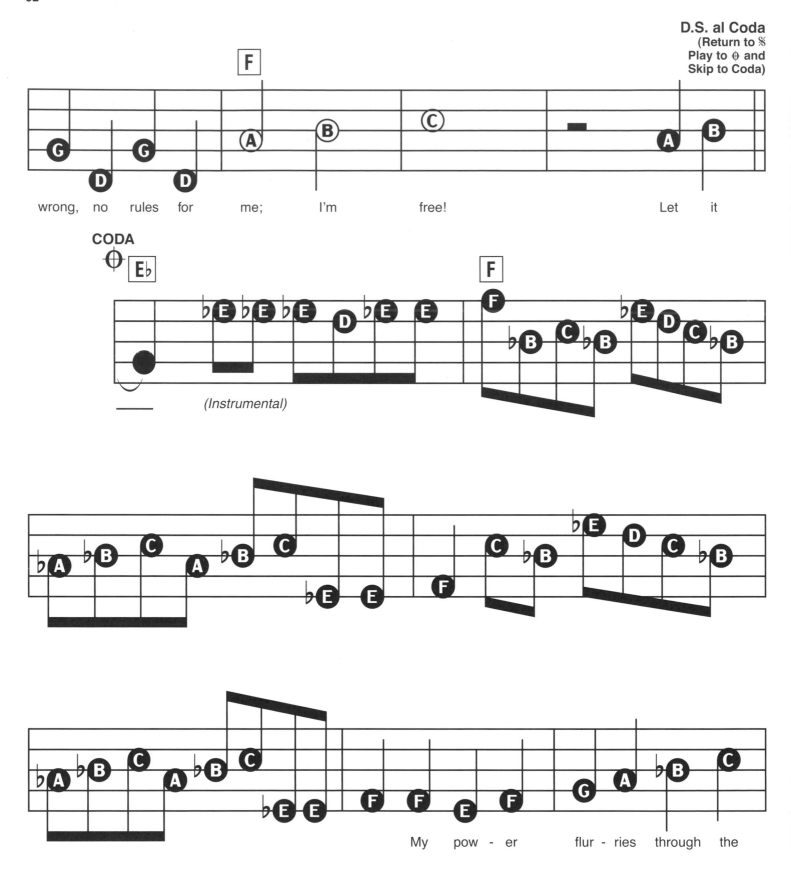

wrong, no rules for me; I'm free! Let it

CODA

(Instrumental)

My pow - er flur - ries through the

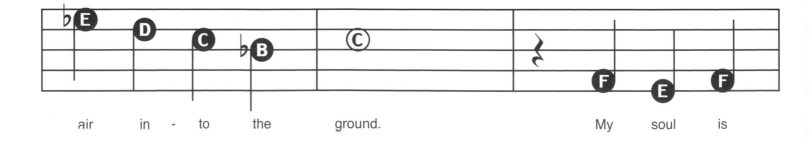

air in - to the ground. My soul is

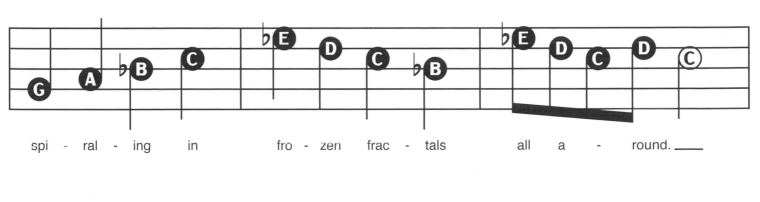

spi - ral - ing in fro - zen frac - tals all a - round. ___

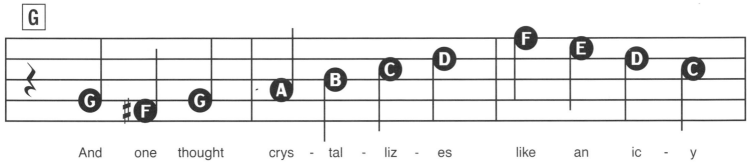

And one thought crys - tal - liz - es like an ic - y

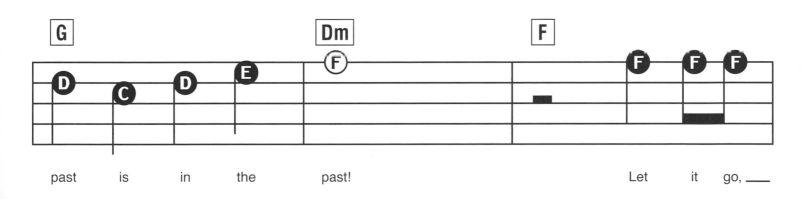

blast: I'm nev - er go - ing back; the

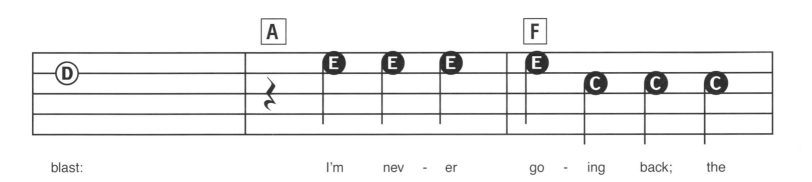

past is in the past! Let it go, ___

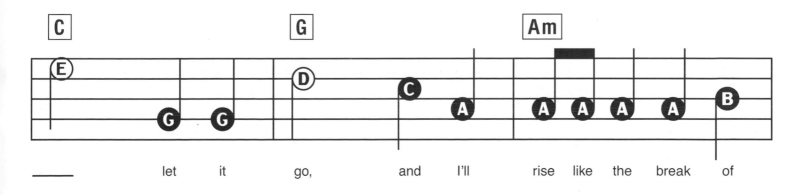

___ let it go, and I'll rise like the break of

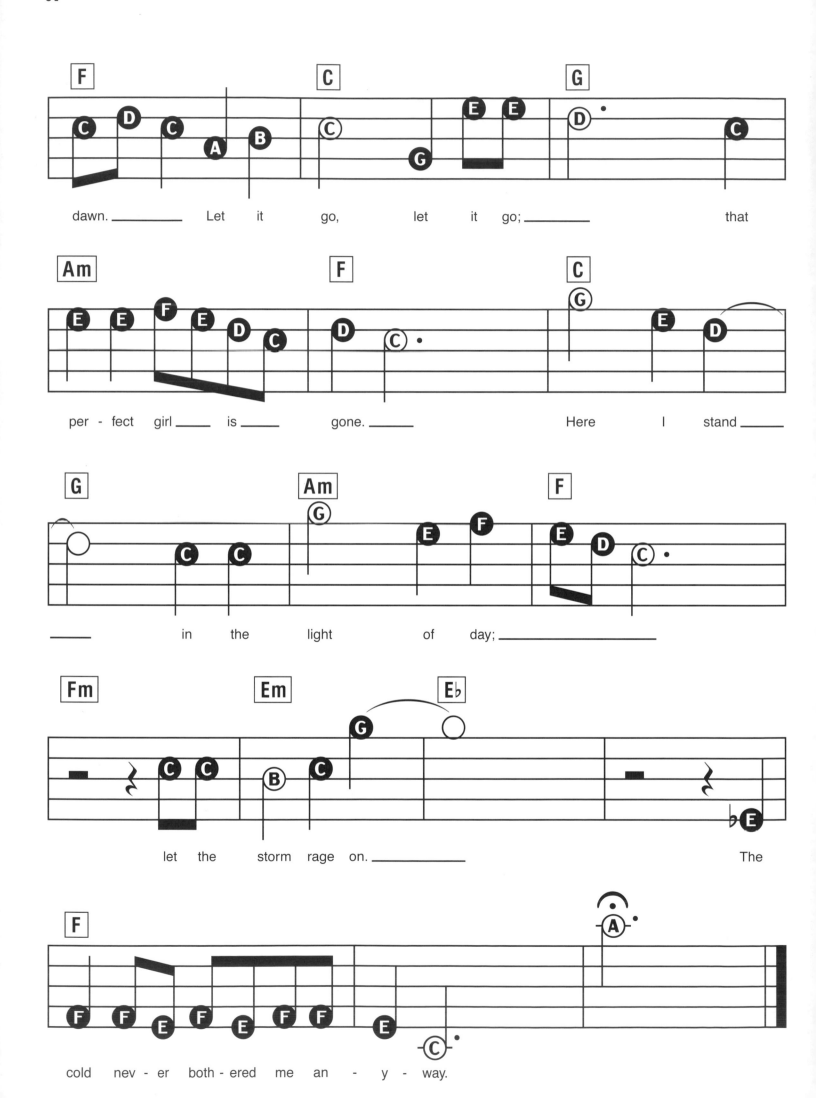

Radioactive

Registration 4
Rhythm: 8-Beat or Rock

Words and Music by Daniel Reynolds,
Benjamin McKee, Daniel Sermon,
Alexander Grant and Josh Mosser

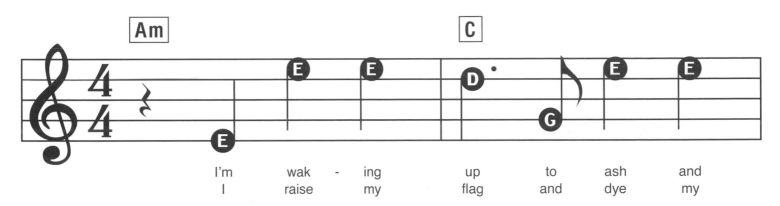

I'm wak - ing up to ash and
I raise my flag and dye my

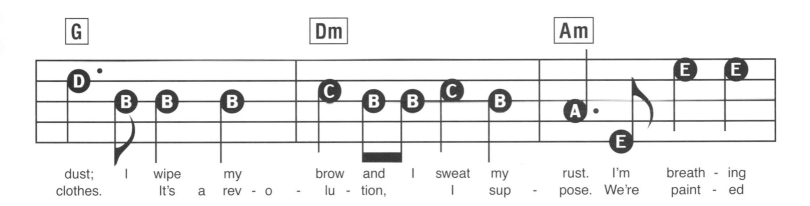

dust; I wipe my brow and I sweat my rust. I'm breath - ing
clothes. It's a rev - o - lu - tion, I sup - pose. We're paint - ed

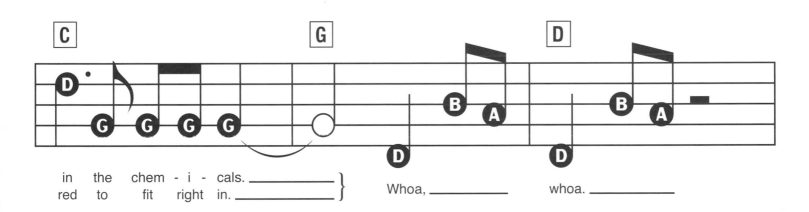

in the chem - i - cals. _____
red to fit right in. _____ }

Whoa, _____ whoa. _____

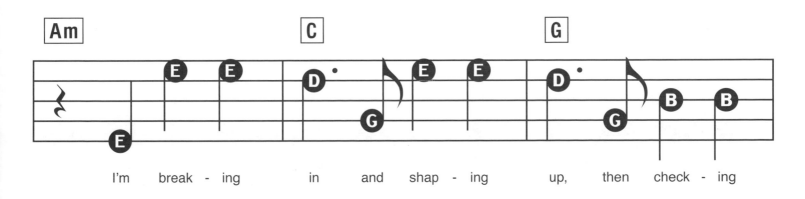

I'm break - ing in and shap - ing up, then check - ing

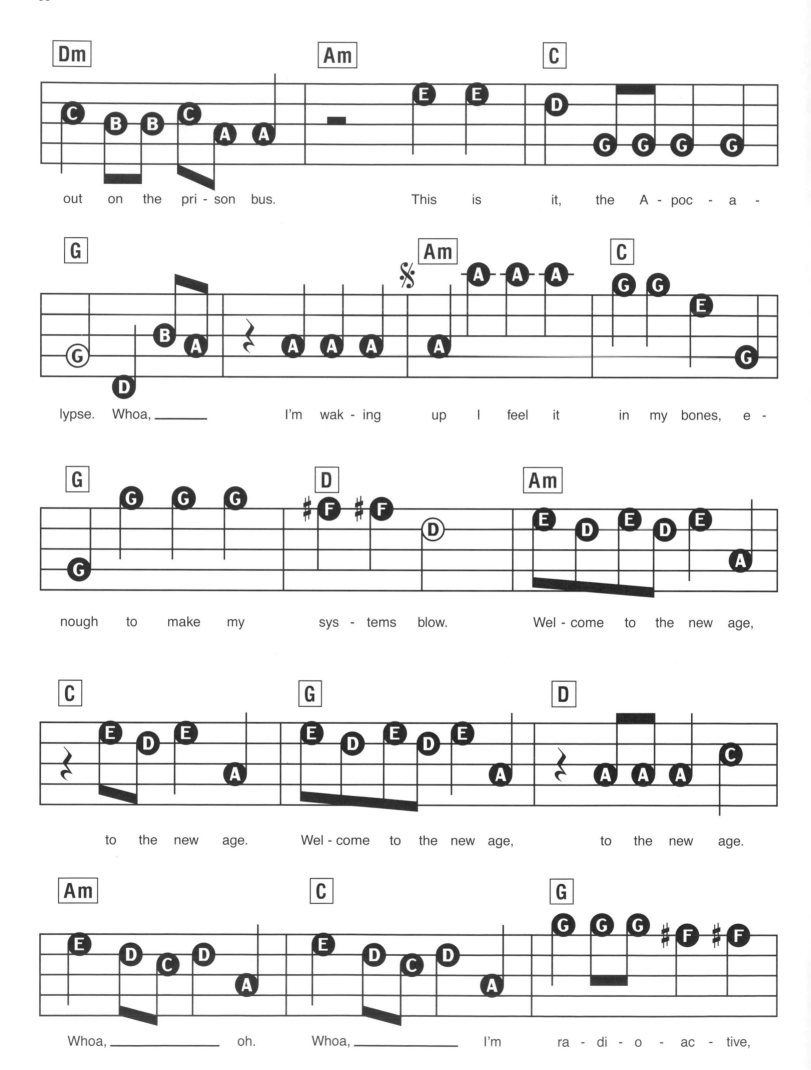

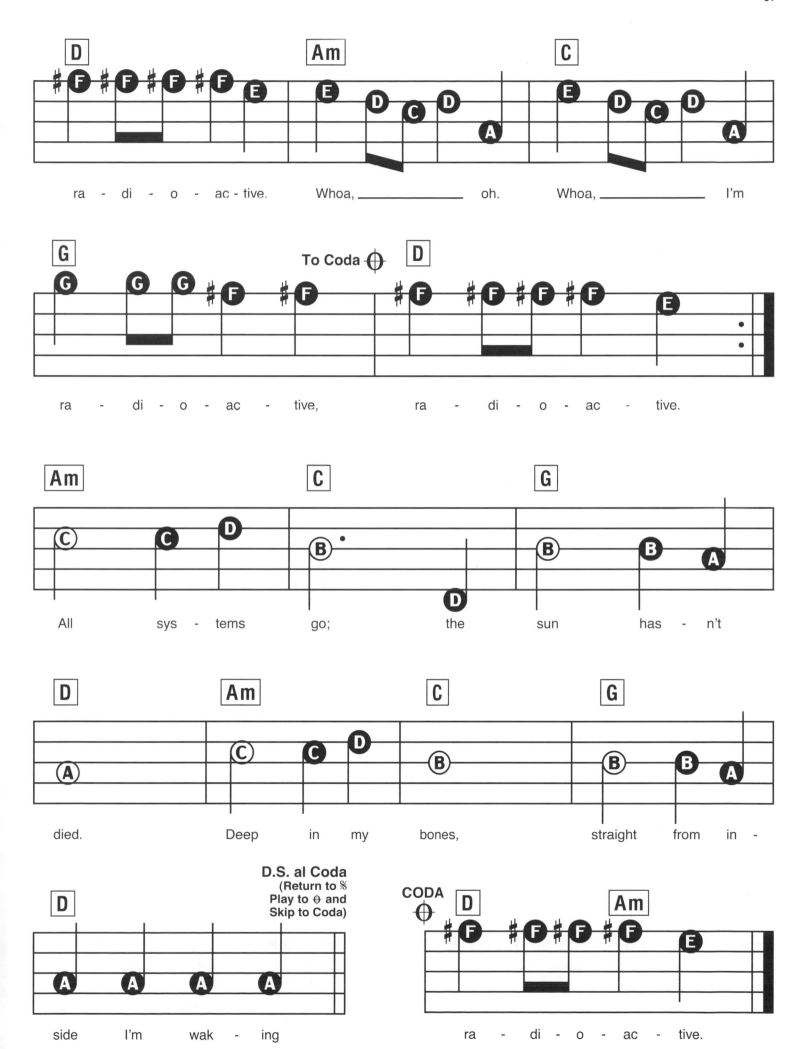

Mean

Registration 4
Rhythm: Bluegrass or Fox Trot

Words and Music by
Taylor Swift

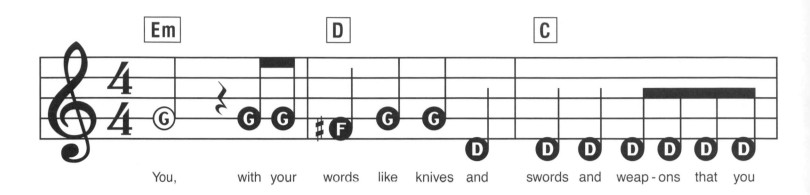

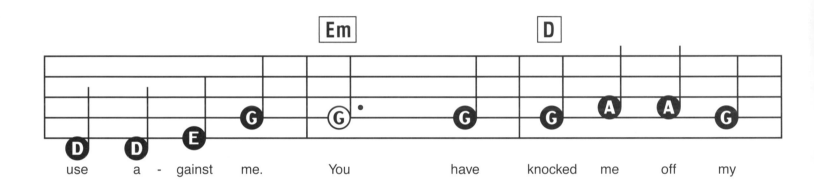

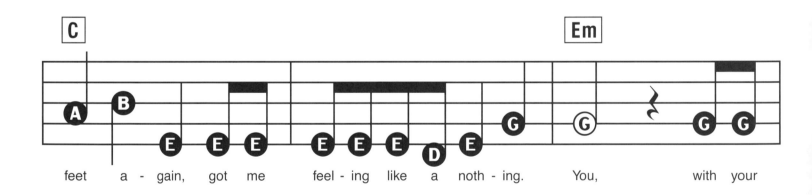

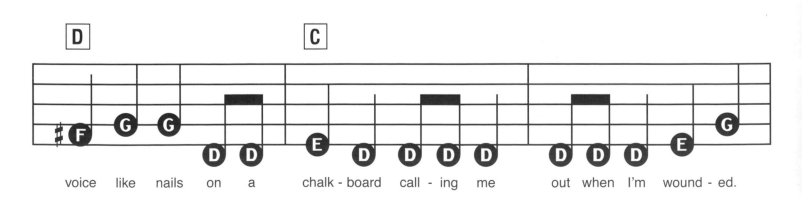

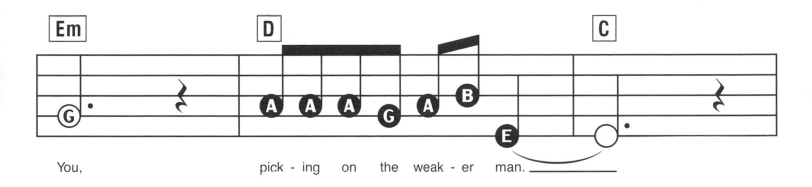

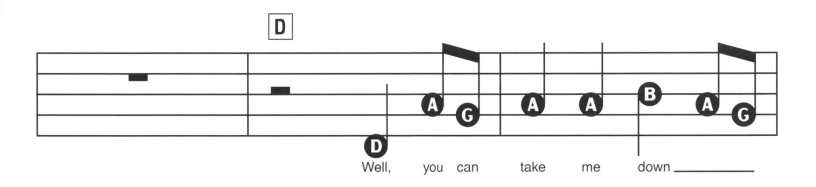

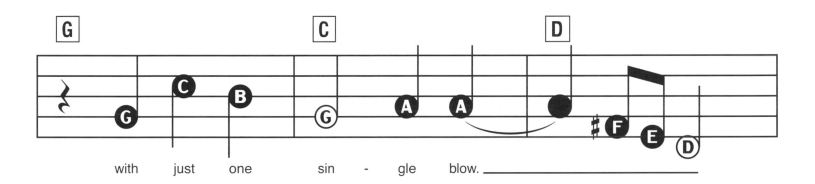

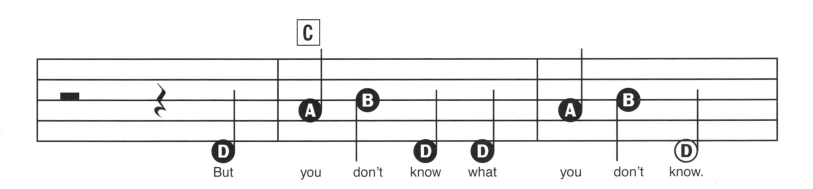

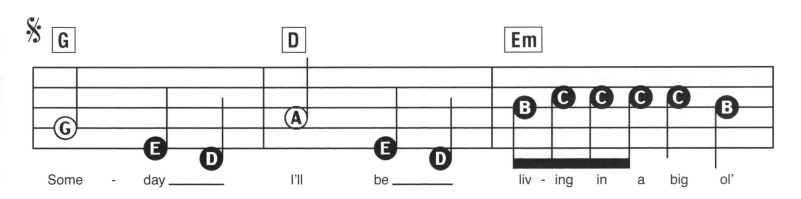

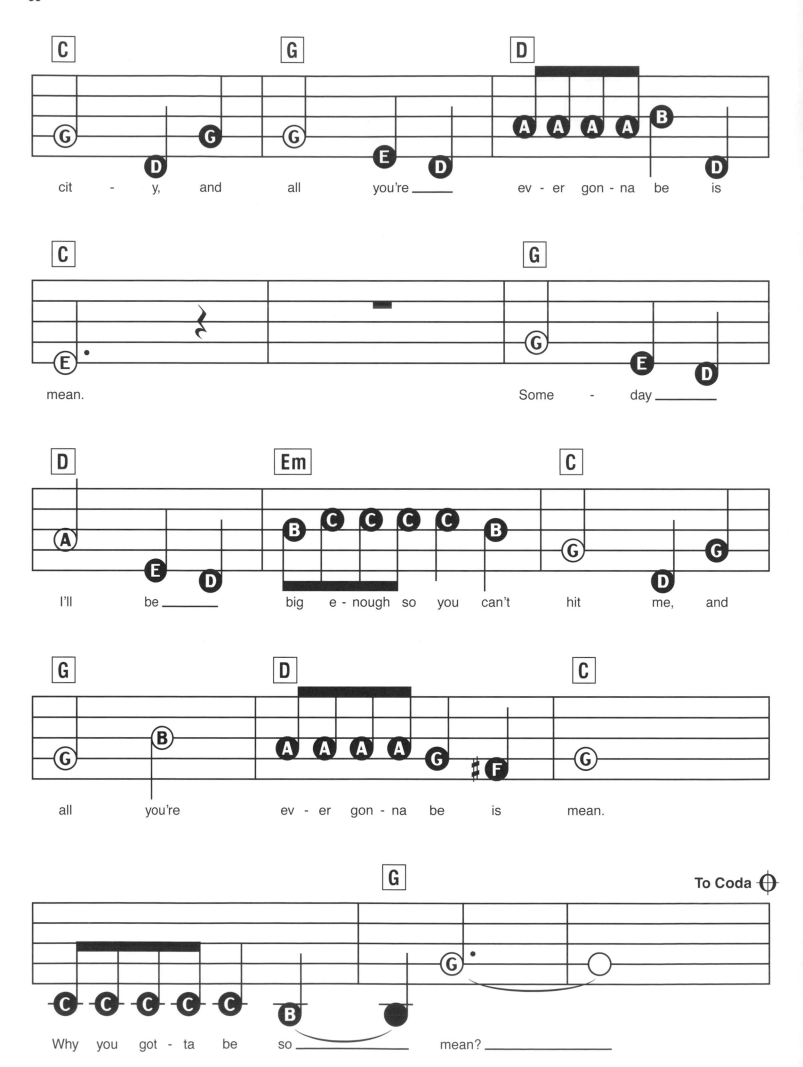

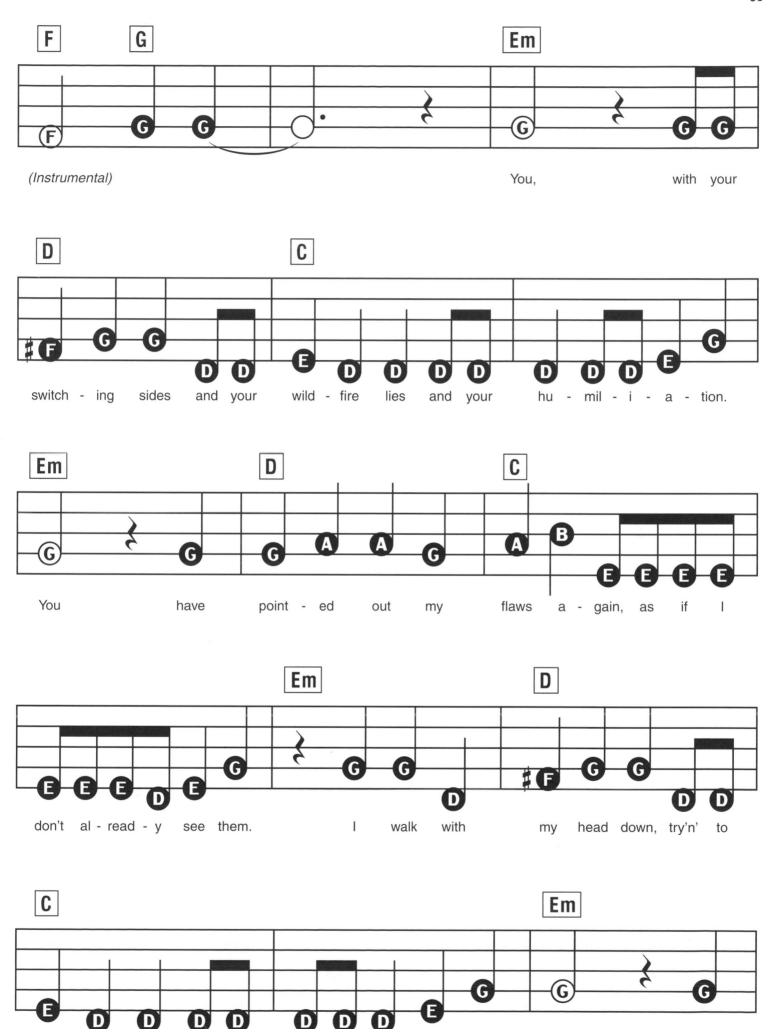

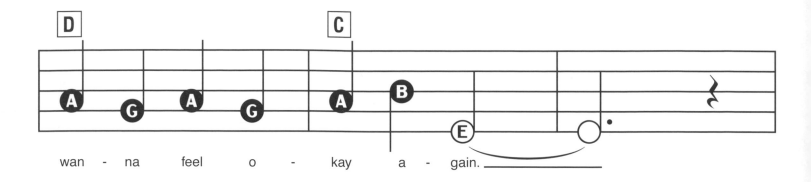

wan - na feel o - kay a - gain. _____

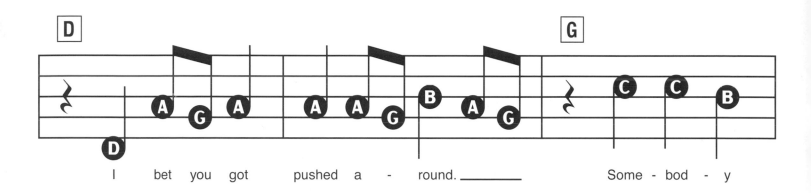

I bet you got pushed a - round. _____ Some - bod - y

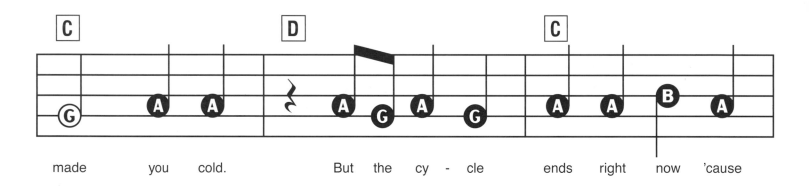

made you cold. But the cy - cle ends right now 'cause

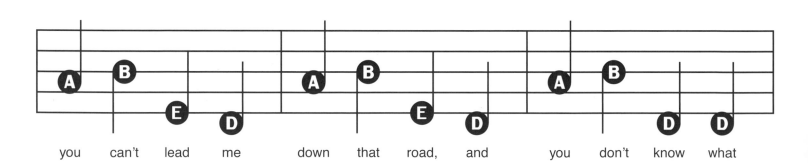

you can't lead me down that road, and you don't know what

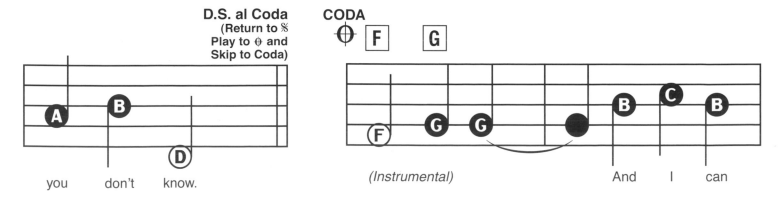

D.S. al Coda
(Return to 𝄋
Play to ⨁ and
Skip to Coda)

CODA

you don't know.

(Instrumental) And I can

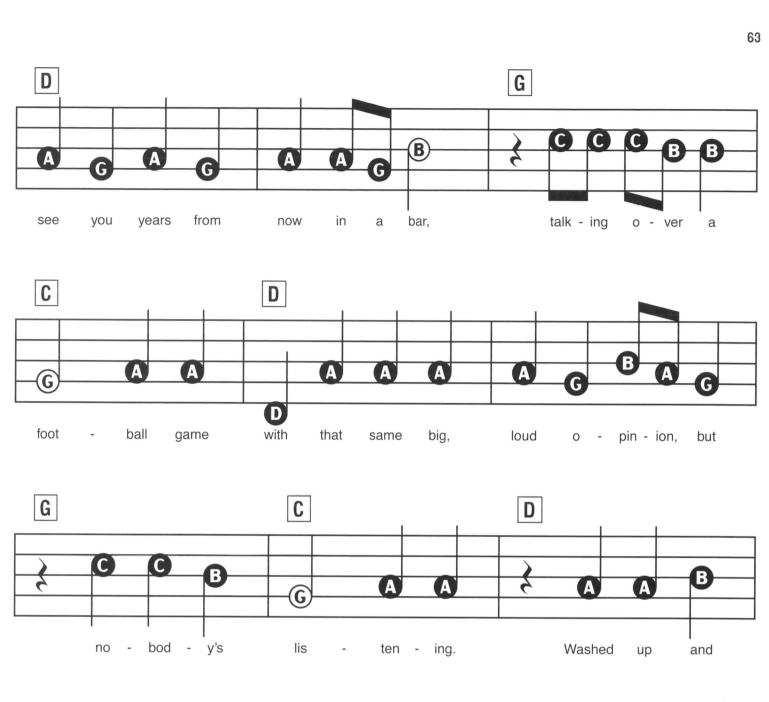

see you years from now in a bar, talk - ing o - ver a

foot - ball game with that same big, loud o - pin - ion, but

no - bod - y's lis - ten - ing. Washed up and

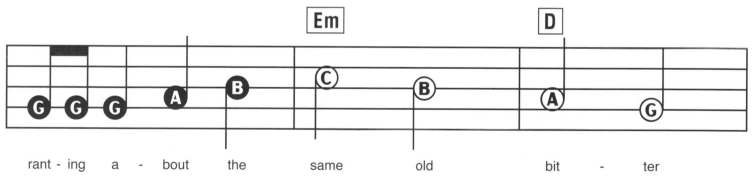

rant - ing a - bout the same old bit - ter

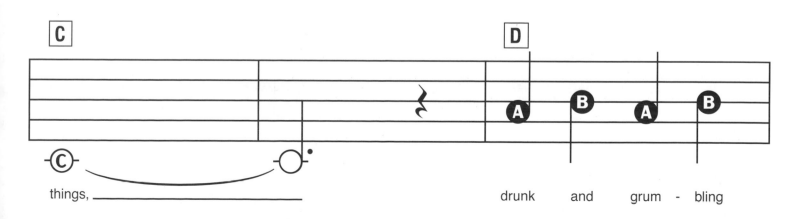

things, _____ drunk and grum - bling

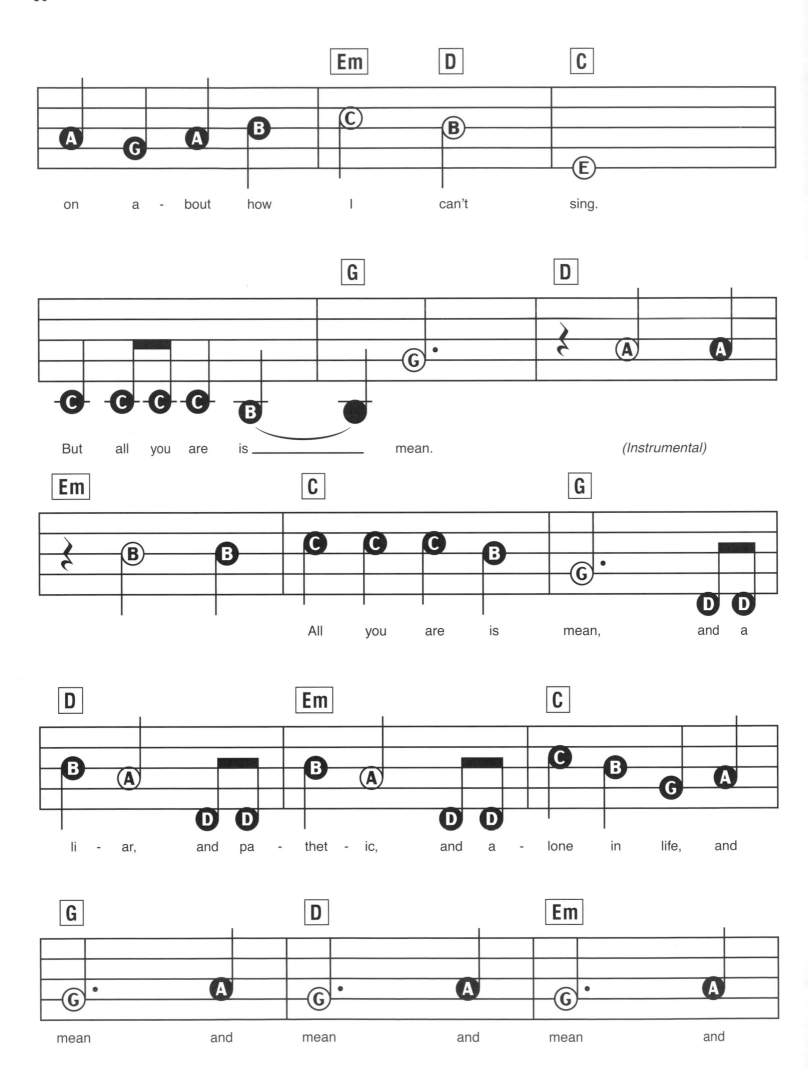

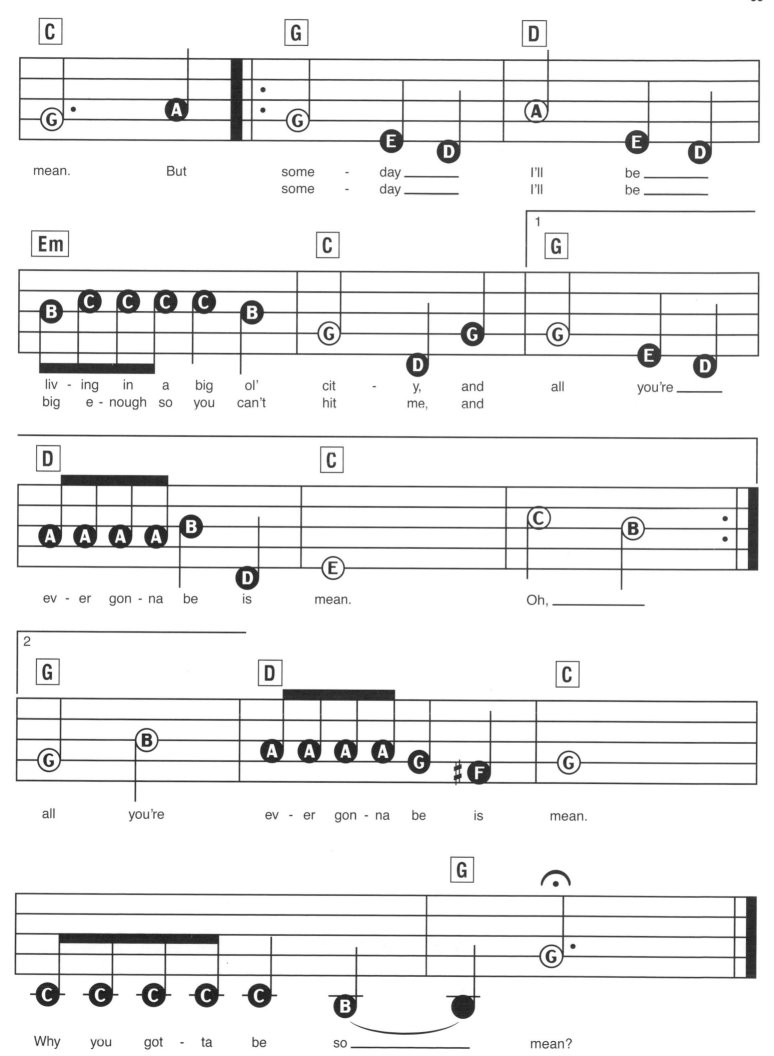

Roar

Registration 1
Rhythm: 8-Beat or Rock

Words and Music by Katy Perry,
Lukasz Gottwald, Max Martin,
Bonnie McKee and Henry Walter

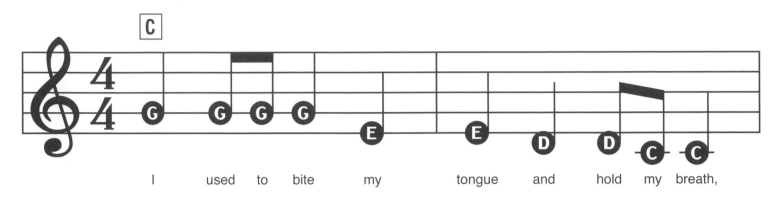

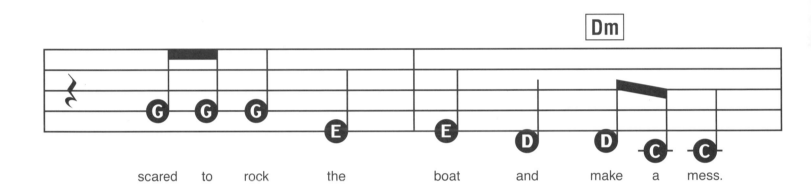

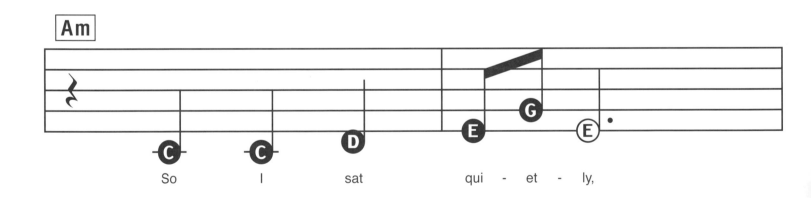

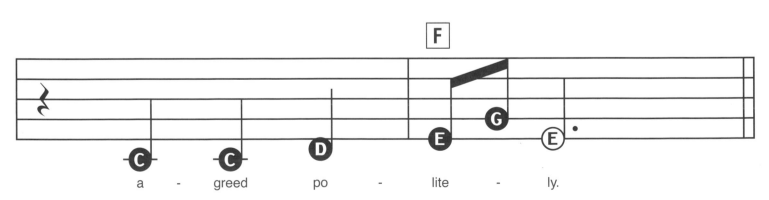

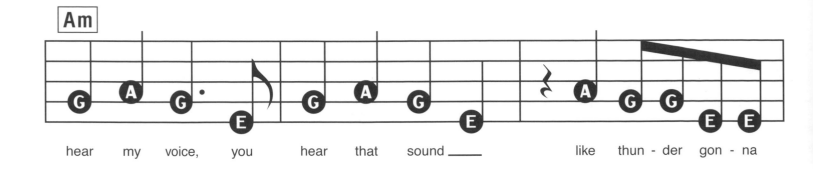

hear my voice, you hear that sound ___ like thun - der gon - na

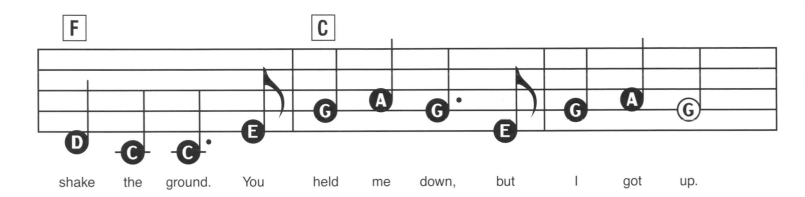

shake the ground. You held me down, but I got up.

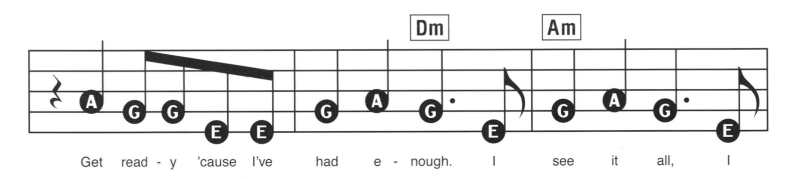

Get read - y 'cause I've had e - nough. I see it all, I

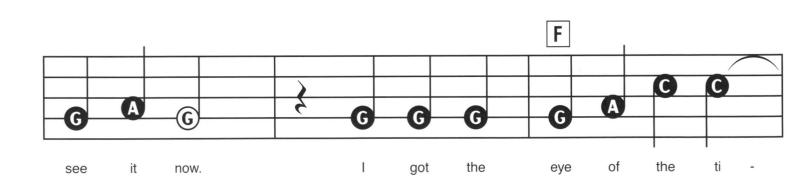

see it now. I got the eye of the ti -

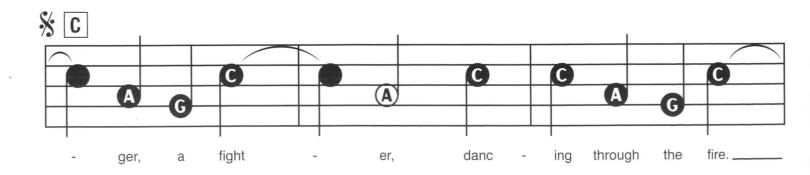

- ger, a fight - er, danc - ing through the fire. ___

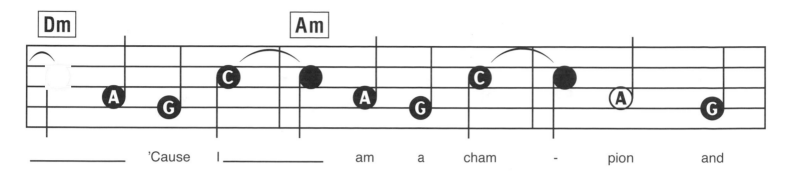
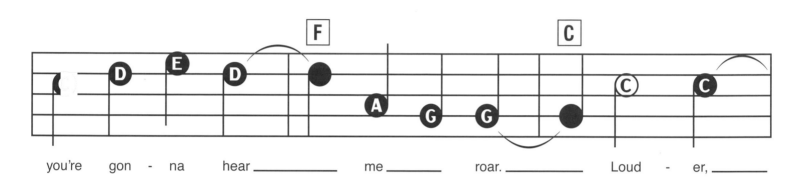
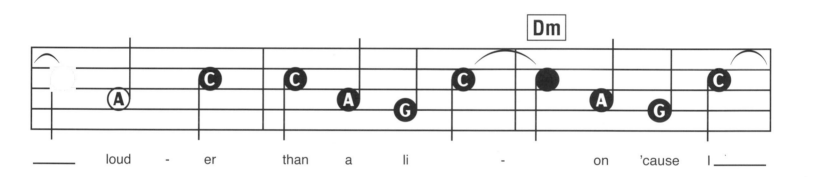
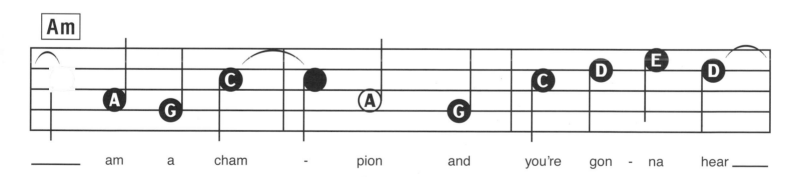
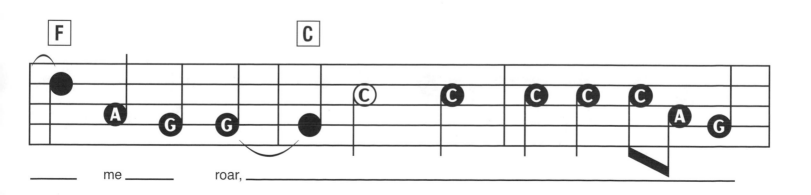

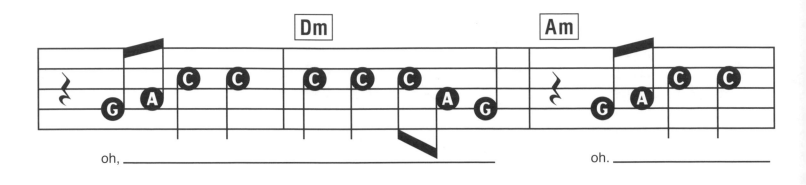

oh, _____ oh. _____

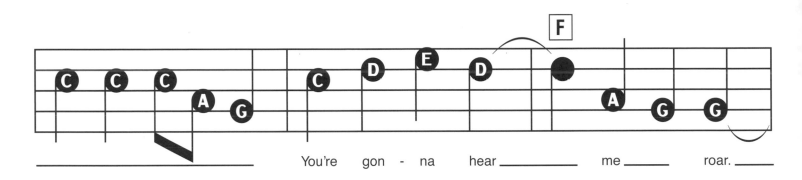

_____ You're gon - na hear _____ me _____ roar. _____

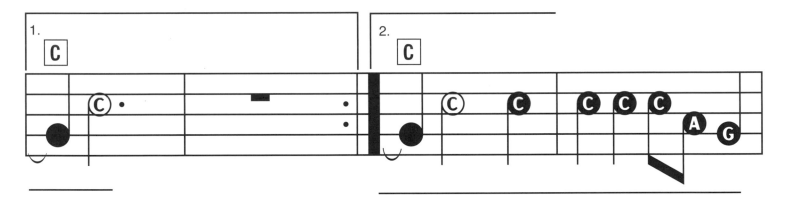

_____

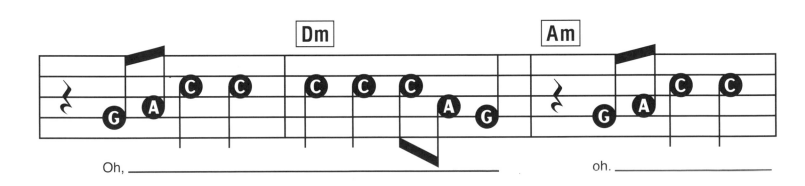

Oh, _____ oh. _____

To Coda ⊕

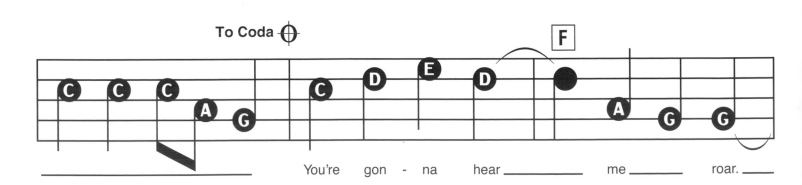

_____ You're gon - na hear _____ me _____ roar. _____

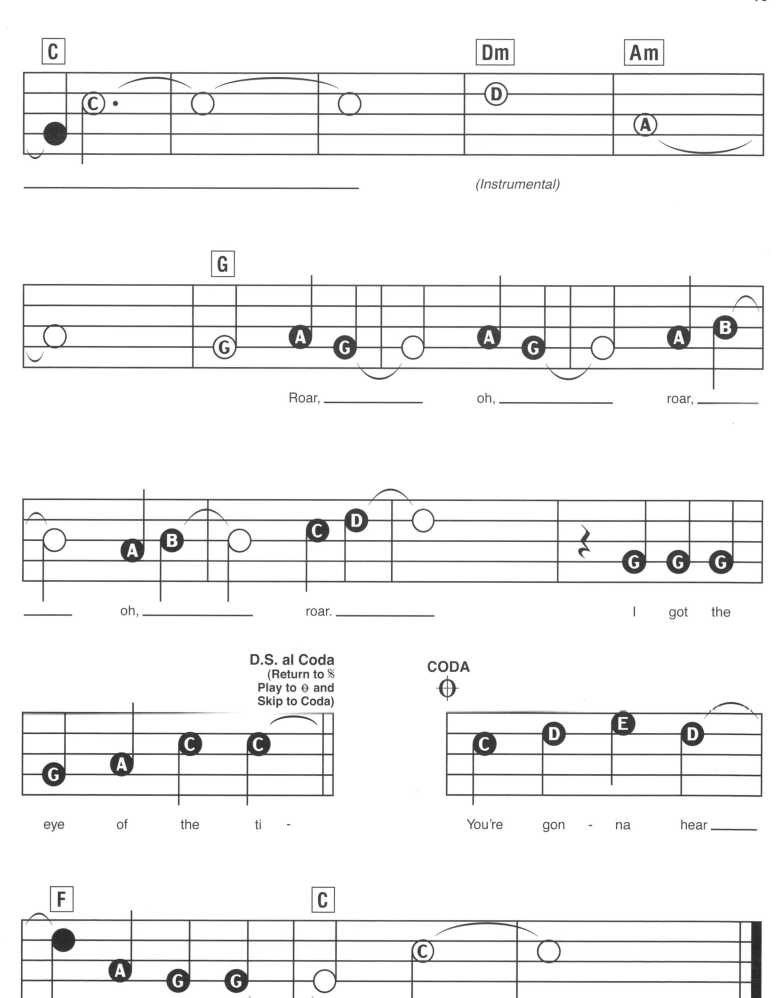

(Instrumental)

Roar, _____ oh, _____ roar, _____

_____ oh, _____ roar. _____ I got the

D.S. al Coda
(Return to 𝄋
Play to ⊕ and
Skip to Coda)

CODA
⊕

eye of the ti -

You're gon - na hear _____

_____ me _____ roar. _____

Royals

Registration 9
Rhythm: 8-Beat or Calypso

Words and Music by Ella Yelich-O'Connor
and Joel Little

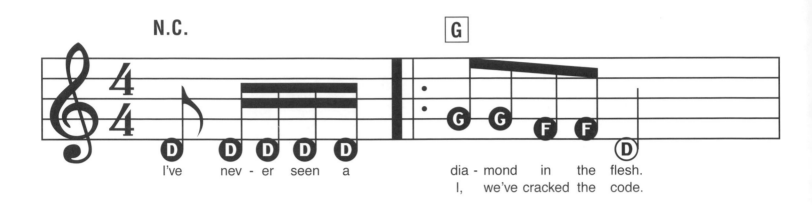

I've nev - er seen a

diamond in the flesh.
I, we've cracked the code.

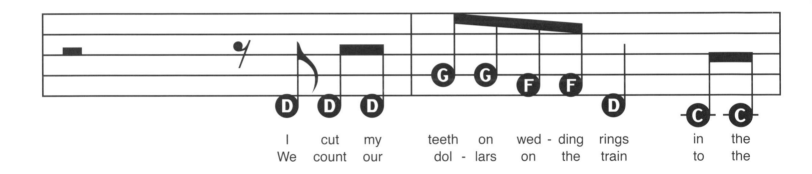

I cut my teeth on wed - ding rings in the
We count our dol - lars on the train to the

mov - ies. _____ And I'm not proud of my ad - dress. _____
par - ty. _____ And ev - 'ry - one who knows us knows _____

In the torn - up town no post - code
that we're fine with this. We did - n't come from

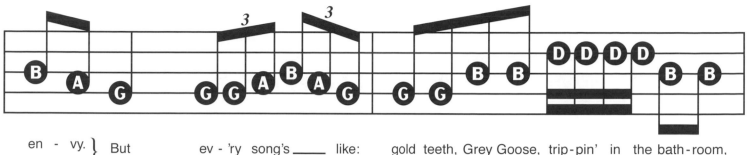

en - vy. } But ev - 'ry song's ___ like: gold teeth, Grey Goose, trip-pin' in the bath-room,
mon - ey. }

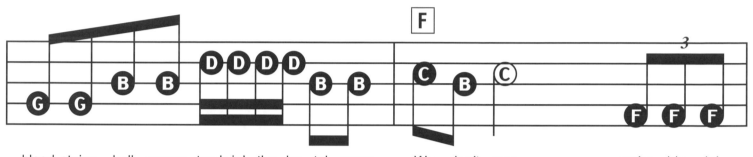

blood stains, ball - gowns, trash-in' the ho - tel room. We don't care, we're driv - in'

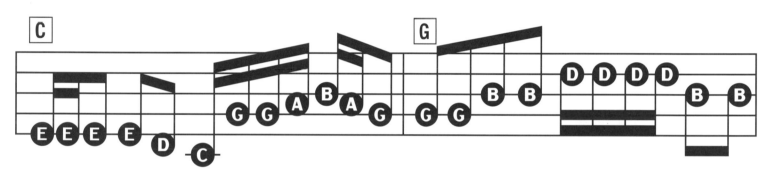

Cad - il - lacs in our dreams. But ev - 'ry - bod - y's like: Cris - tal, May - bach, dia - monds on your time - piece,

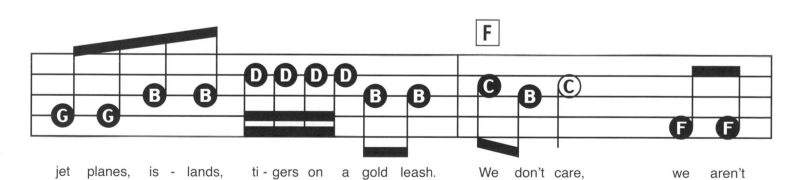

jet planes, is - lands, ti - gers on a gold leash. We don't care, we aren't

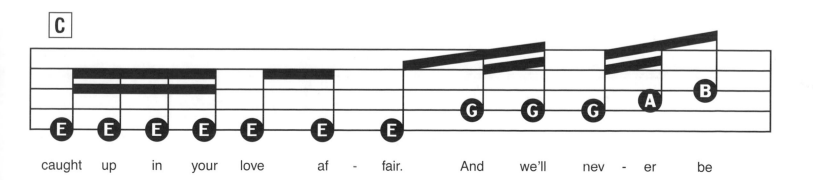

caught up in your love af - fair. And we'll nev - er be

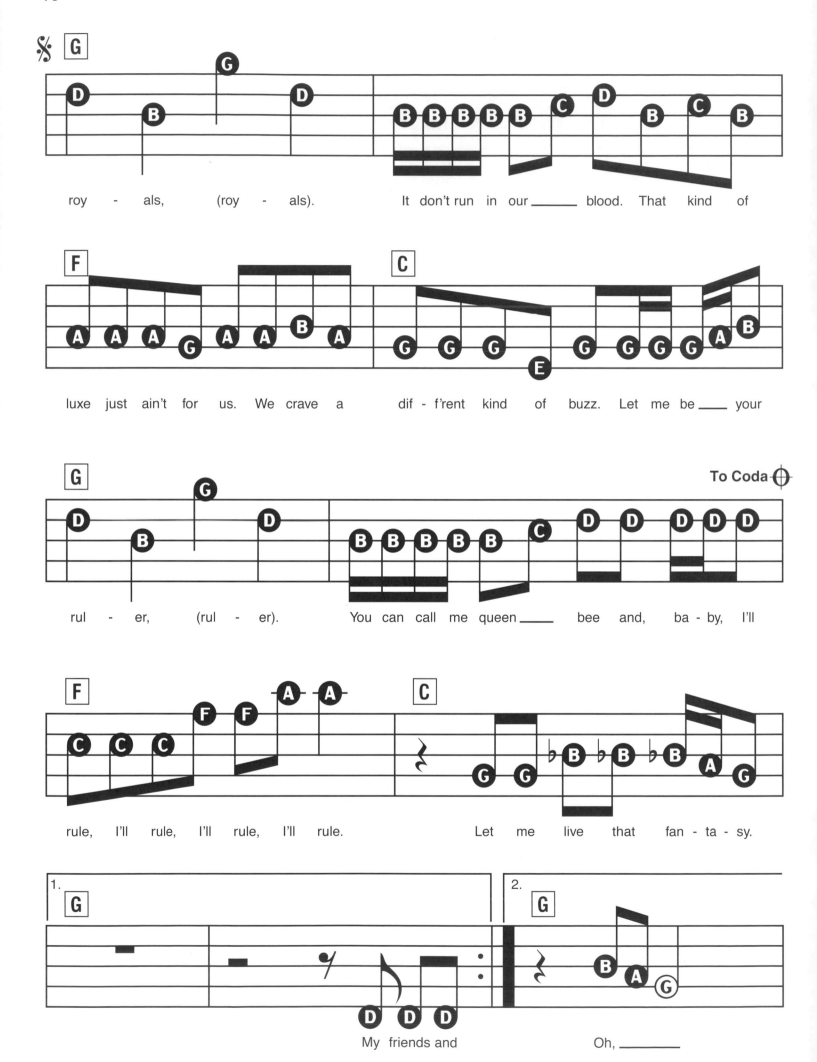

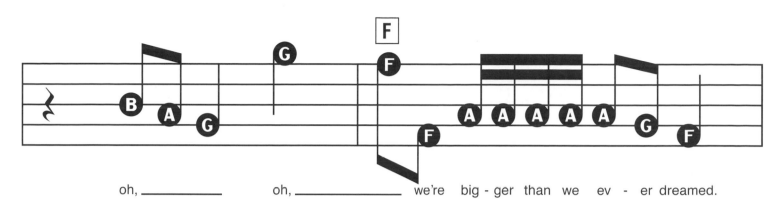

oh, _____ oh, _____ we're big - ger than we ev - er dreamed.

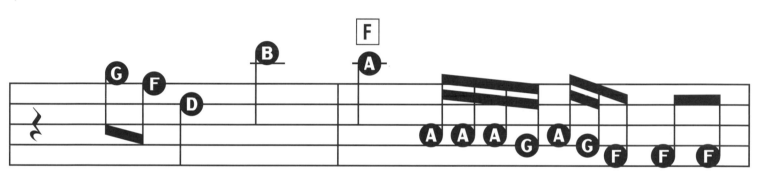

And I'm in love with be - ing queen. Oh, _____

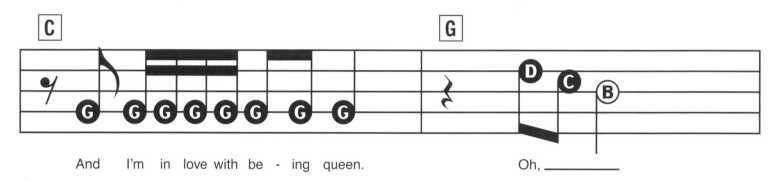

oh, _____ oh, _____ life is game with - out a care. We aren't

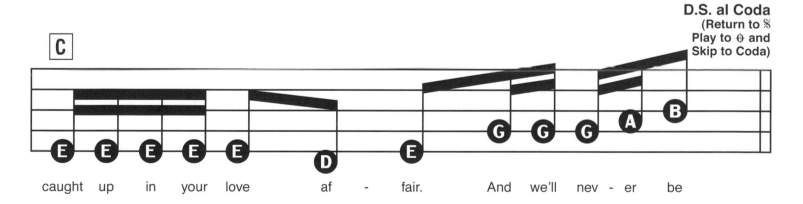

D.S. al Coda
(Return to 𝄋
Play to ⊕ and
Skip to Coda)

caught up in your love af - fair. And we'll nev - er be

CODA

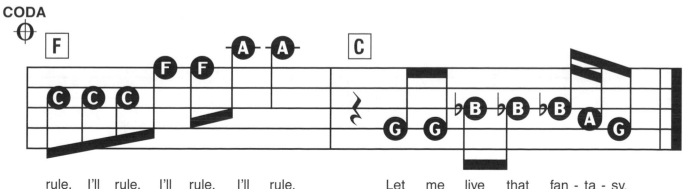

rule, I'll rule, I'll rule, I'll rule. Let me live that fan - ta - sy.

Say Something

Registration 8
Rhythm: Waltz

Words and Music by Ian Axel,
Chad Vaccarino and Mike Campbell

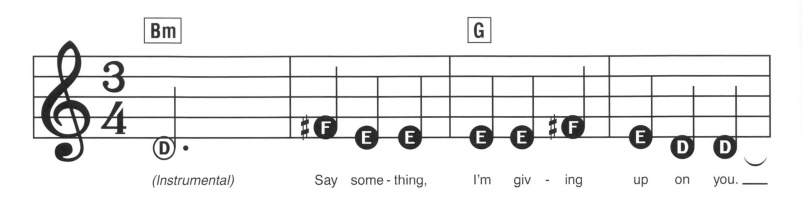

(Instrumental)   Say some - thing,   I'm giv - ing   up on you. ____

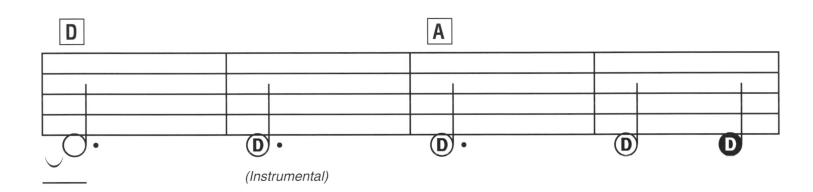

____   (Instrumental)

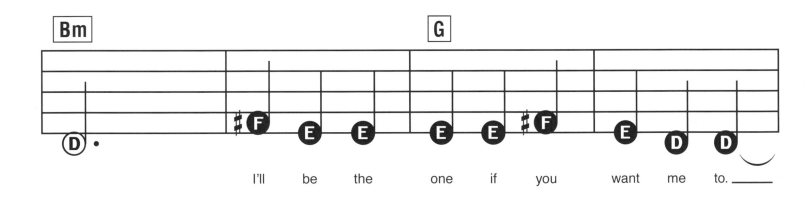

I'll   be   the   one   if   you   want   me   to. ____

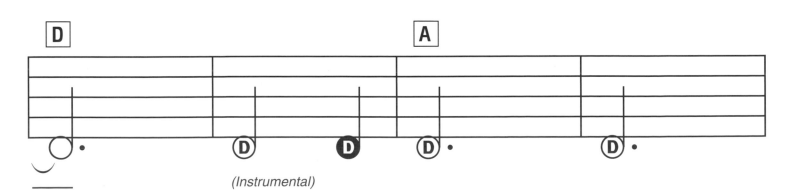

____   (Instrumental)

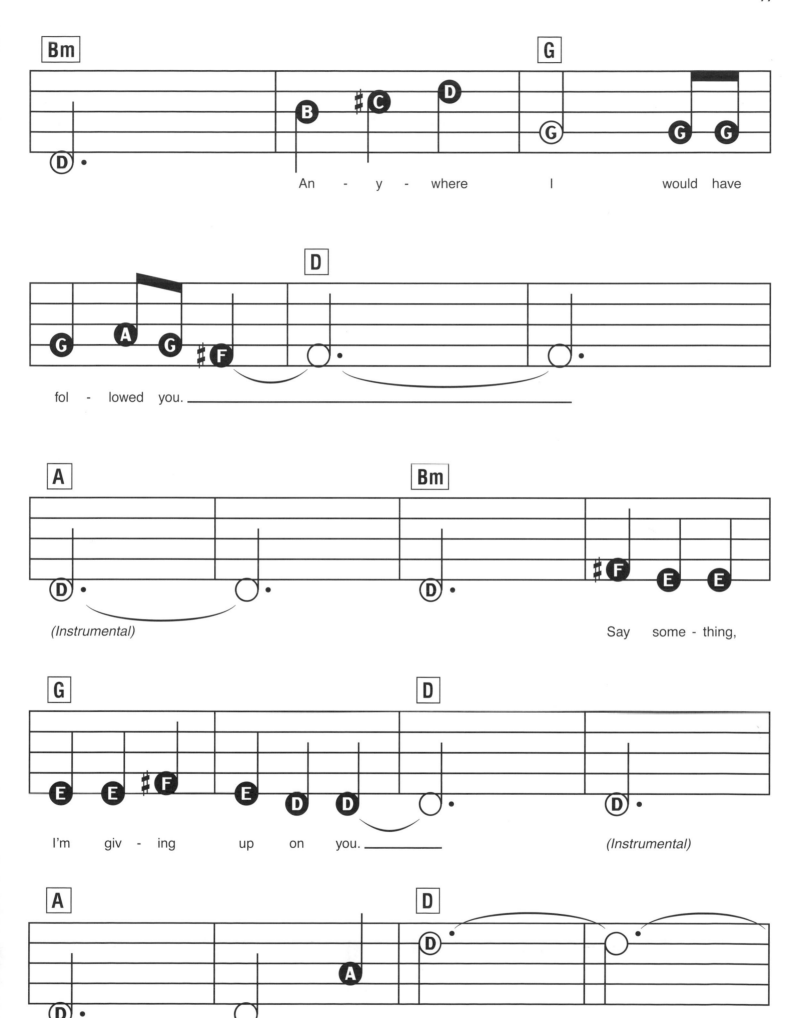

78

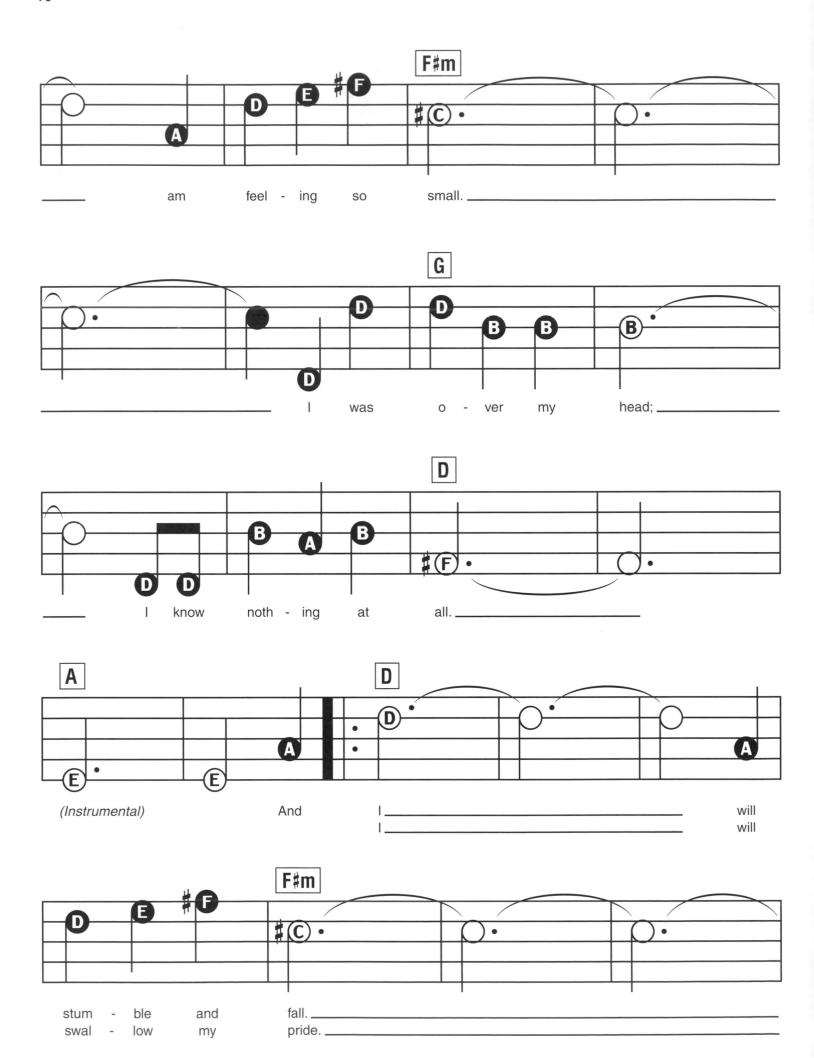

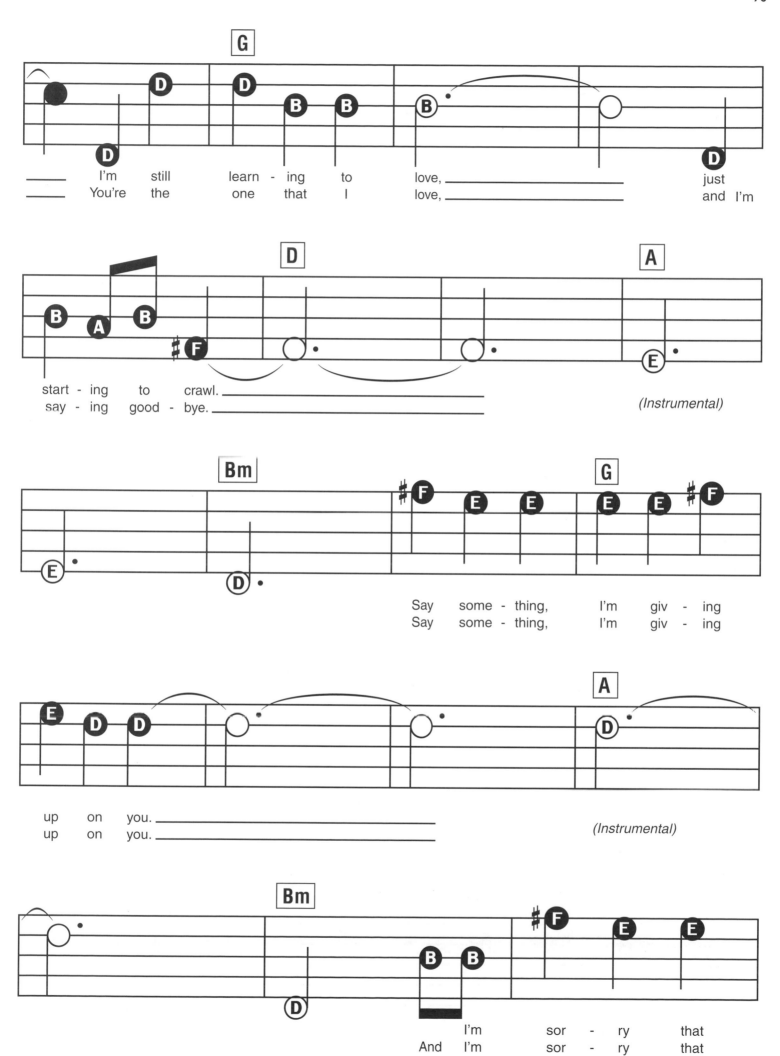

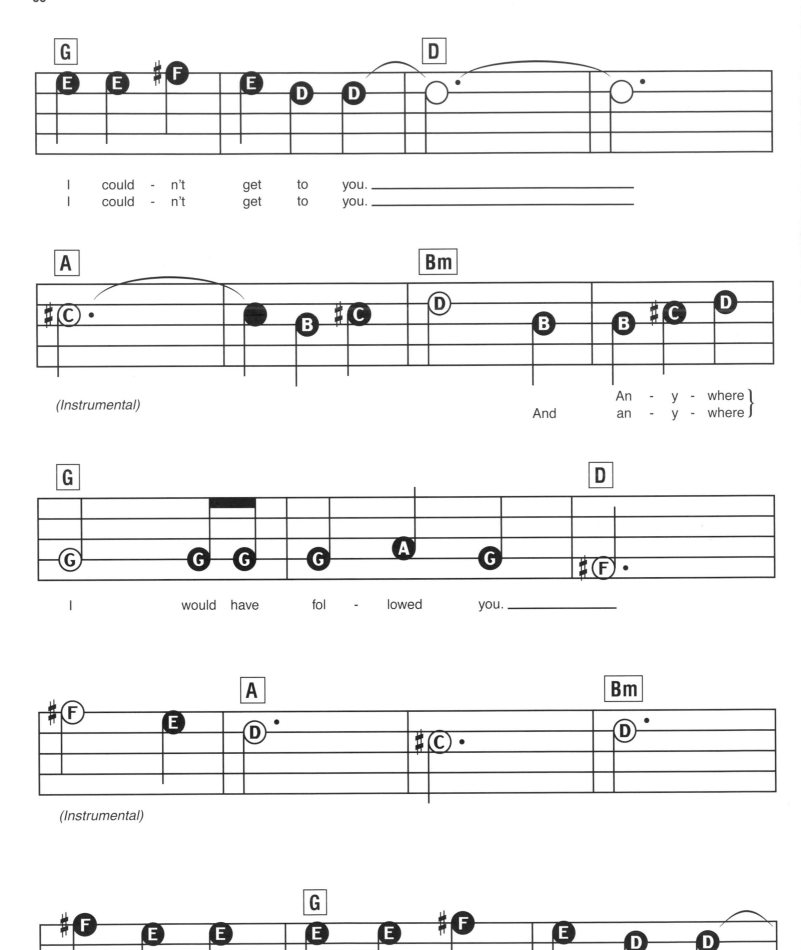

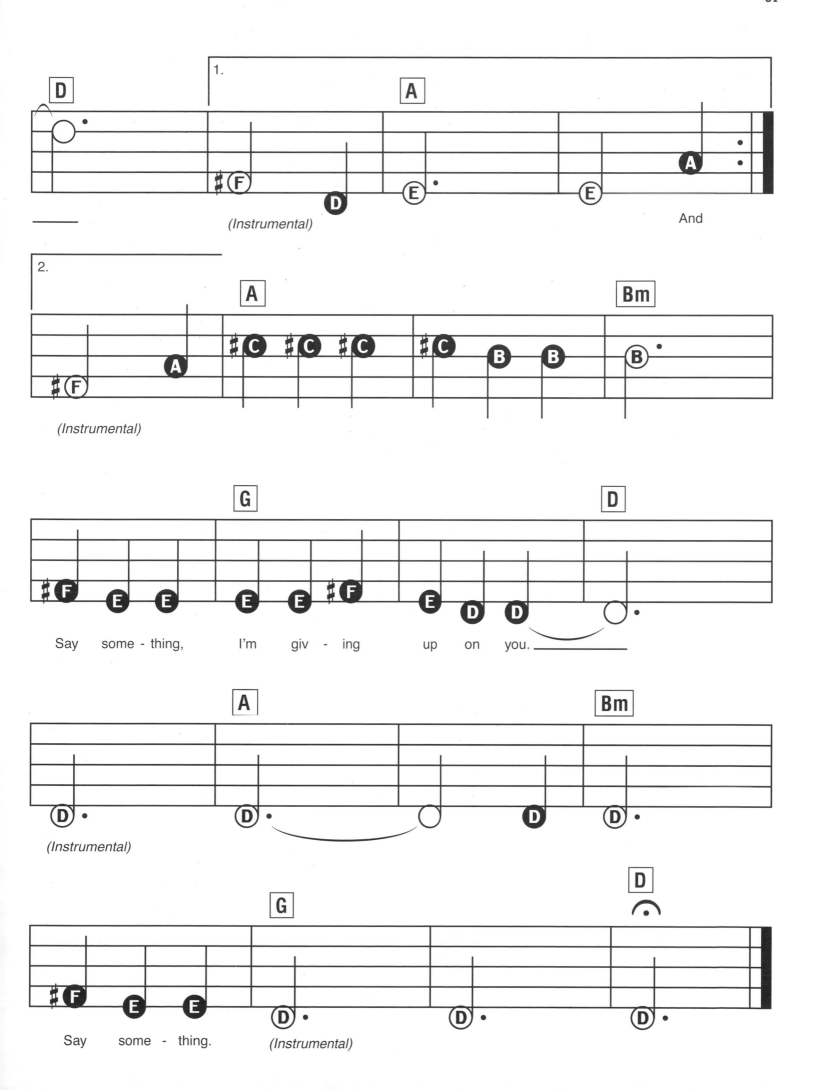

Skyfall
from the Motion Picture SKYFALL

Registration 8
Rhythm: 8-Beat or Ballad

Words and Music by Adele Adkins
and Paul Epworth

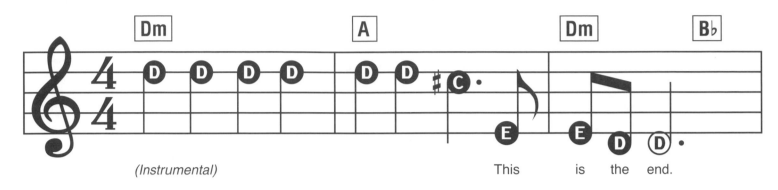

(Instrumental)

This is the end.

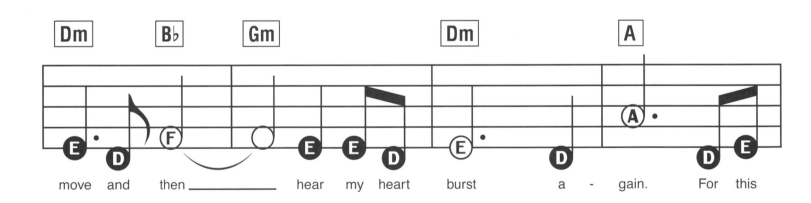

Hold your breath and count to ten. Feel the earth

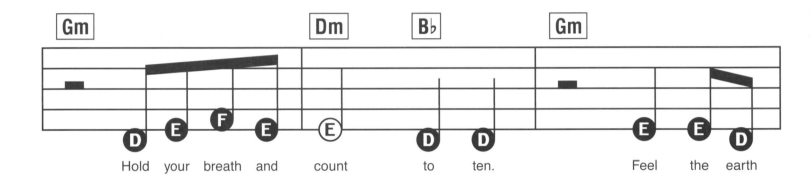

move and then _____ hear my heart burst a - gain. For this

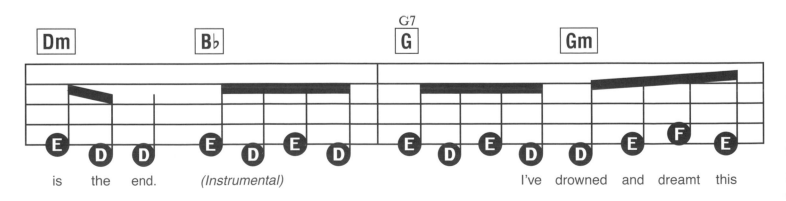

is the end. (Instrumental) I've drowned and dreamt this

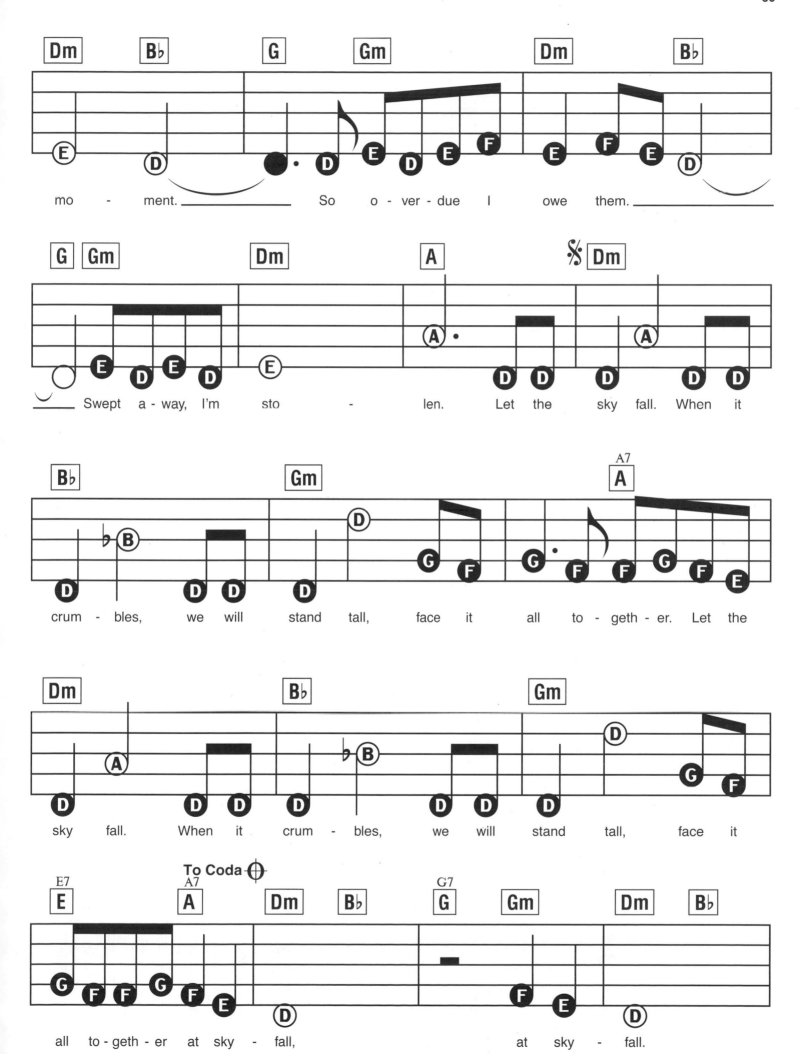

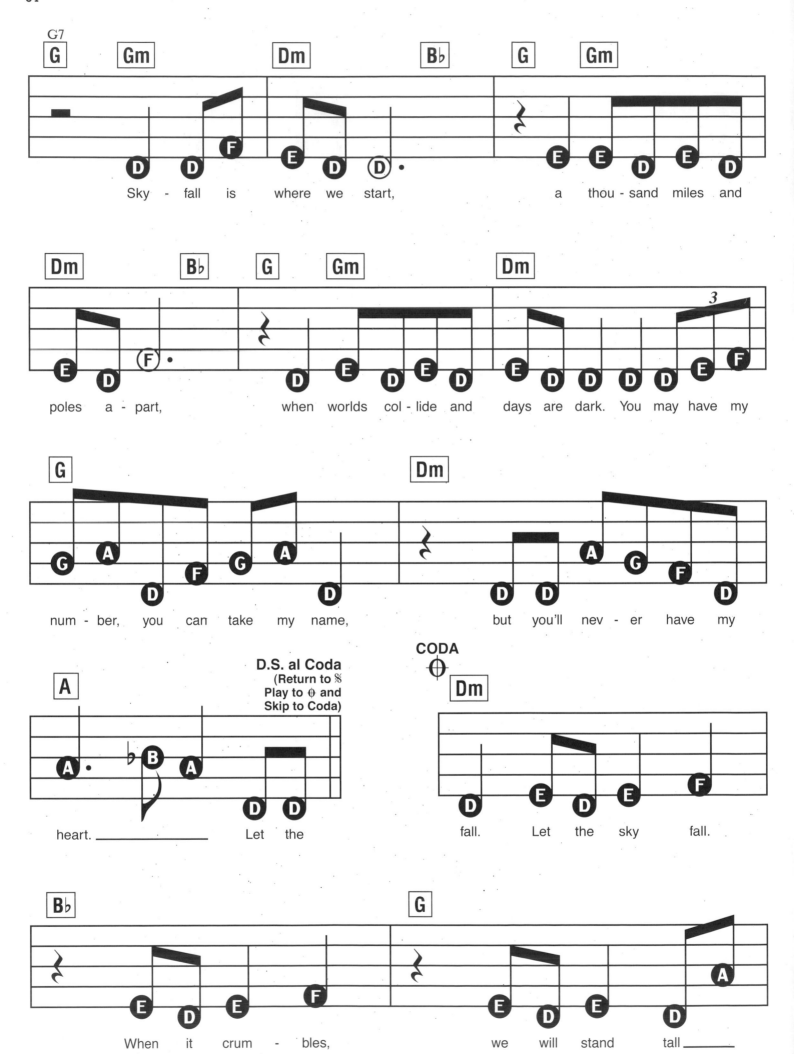

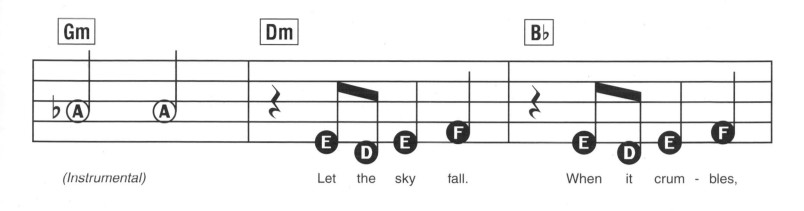

(Instrumental) Let the sky fall. When it crum - bles,

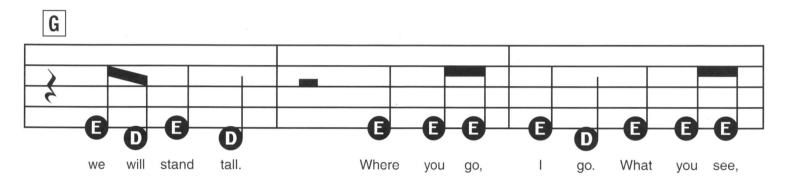

we will stand tall. Where you go, I go. What you see,

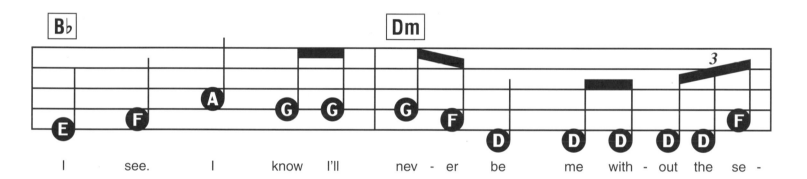

I see. I know I'll nev - er be me with - out the se -

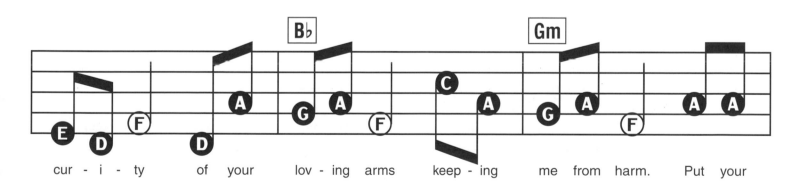

cur - i - ty of your lov - ing arms keep - ing me from harm. Put your

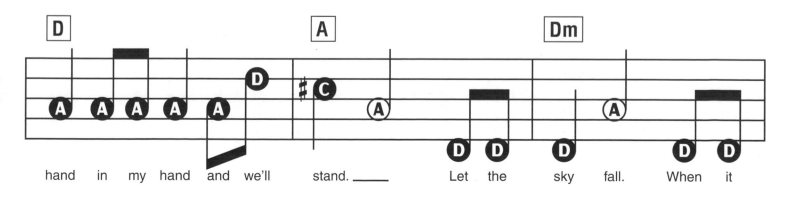

hand in my hand and we'll stand. ____ Let the sky fall. When it

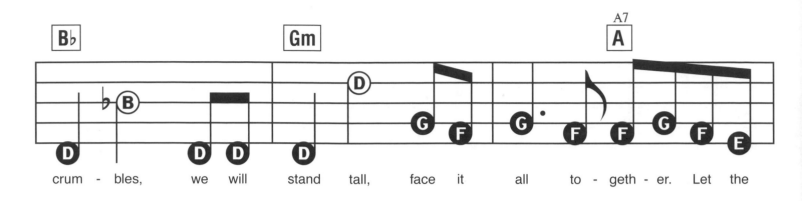

crum - bles, we will stand tall, face it all to - geth - er. Let the

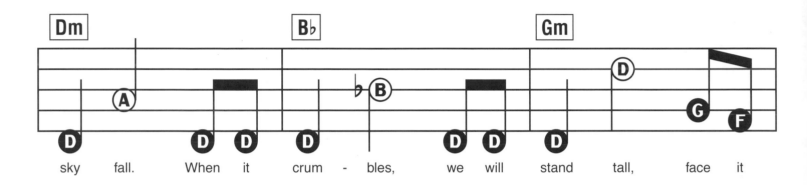

sky fall. When it crum - bles, we will stand tall, face it

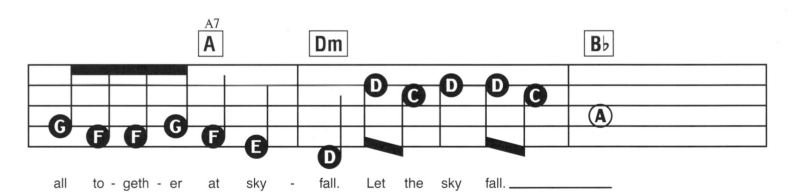

all to - geth - er at sky - fall. Let the sky fall. _____

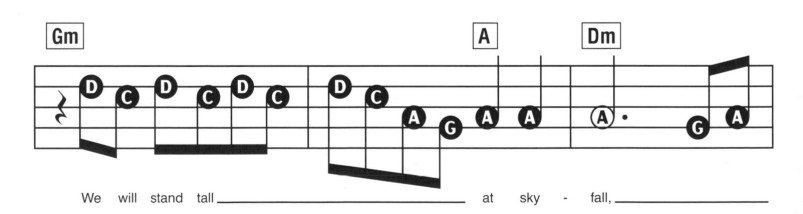

We will stand tall _____ at sky - fall, _____

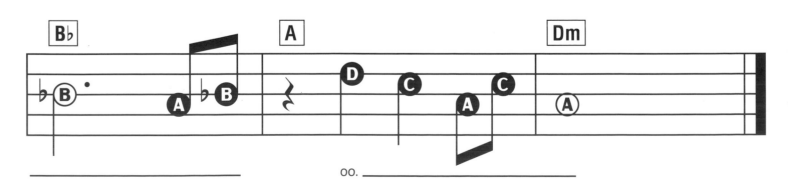

_____ oo. _____

Stay

Registration 8
Rhythm: Ballad

Words and Music by Mikky Ekko
and Justin Parker

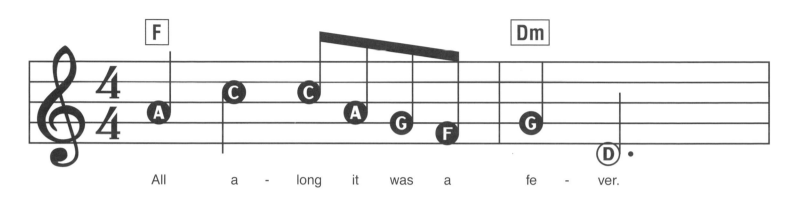

All a - long it was a fe - ver.

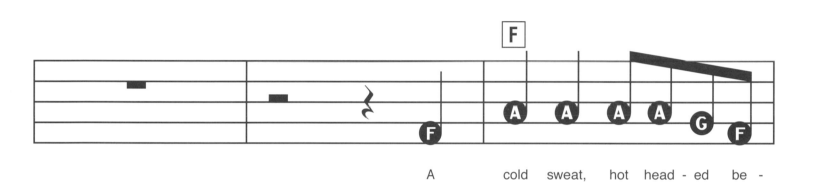

A cold sweat, hot head - ed be -

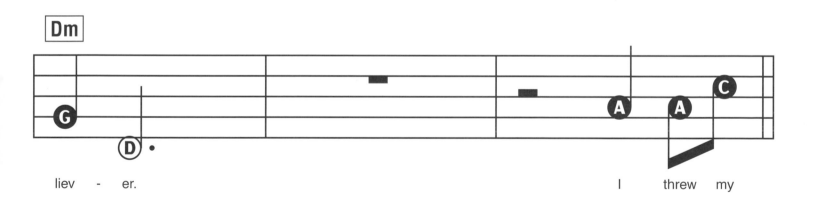

liev - er. I threw my

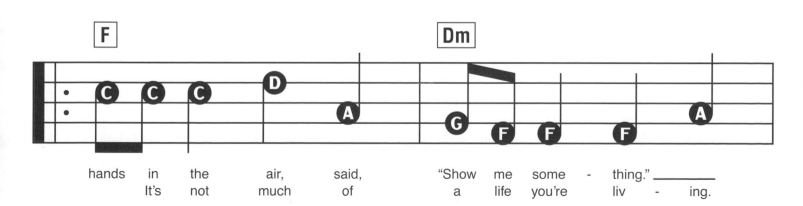

hands in the air, said, "Show me some - thing." _____
It's not much of a life you're liv - ing.

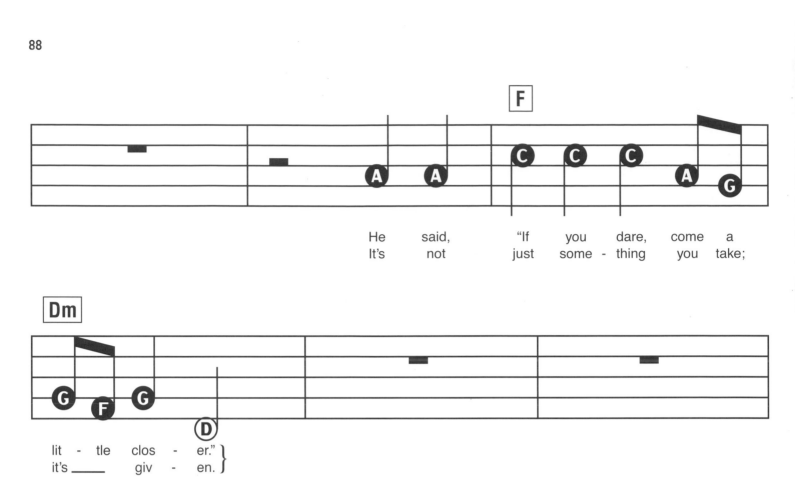

He said,   "If   you   dare,   come   a
It's   not   just   some - thing   you   take;

lit - tle   clos - er."
it's ___   giv - en.

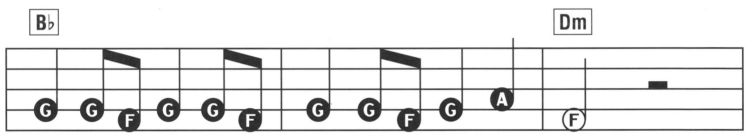

Round   and   a - round   and   a - round   and   a - round   we   go.

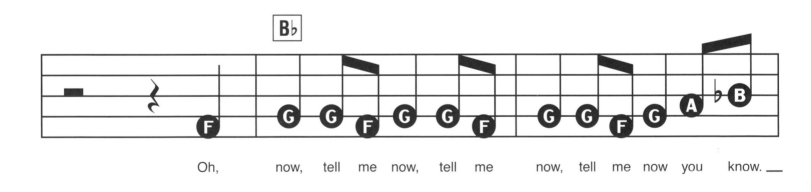

Oh,   now,   tell   me   now,   tell   me   now,   tell   me   now   you   know. ___

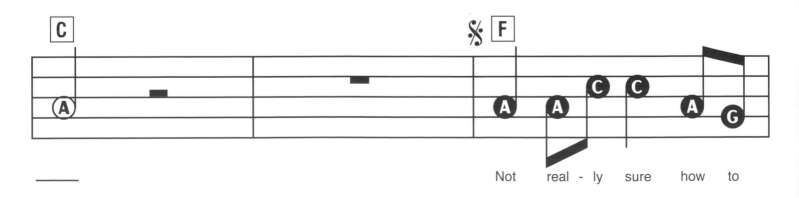

___   Not   real - ly   sure   how   to

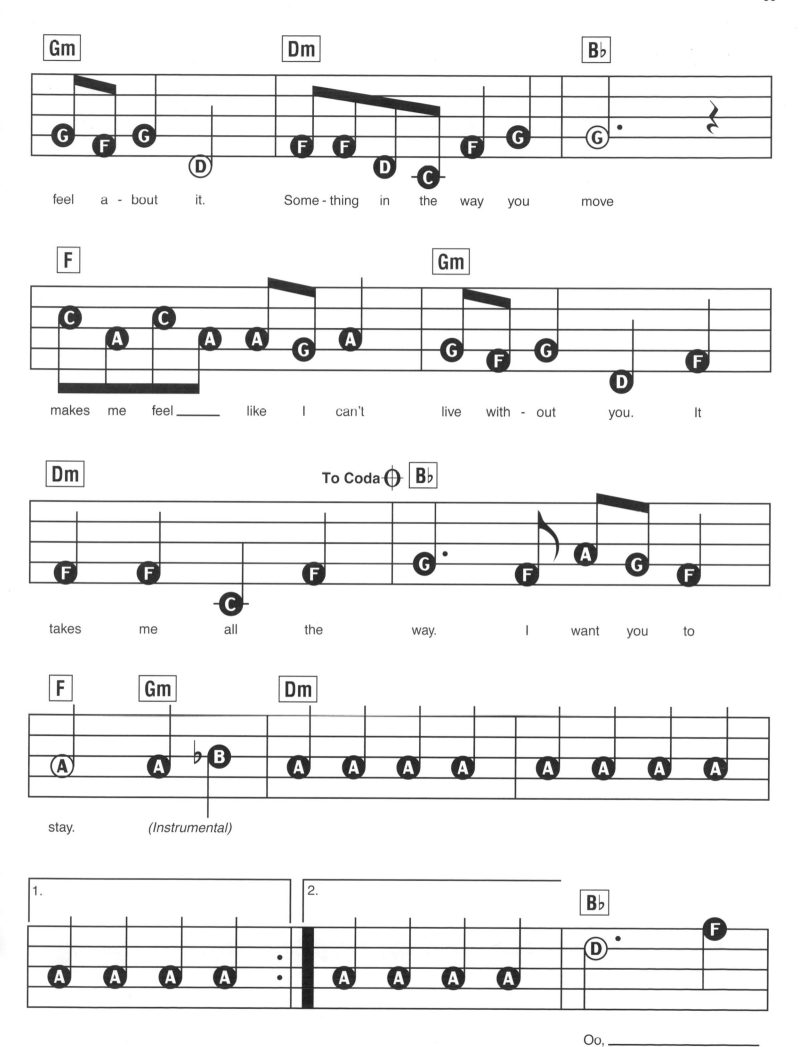

feel a - bout it. Some - thing in the way you move

makes me feel _____ like I can't live with - out you. It

To Coda ✛

takes me all the way. I want you to

stay. *(Instrumental)*

Oo, _____

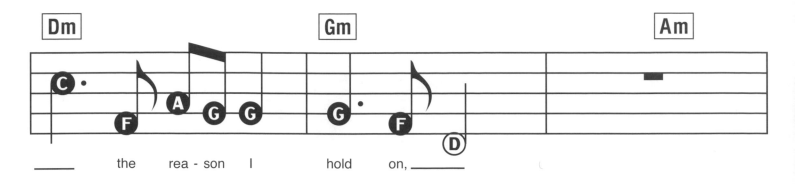

_____ the rea - son I hold on, _____

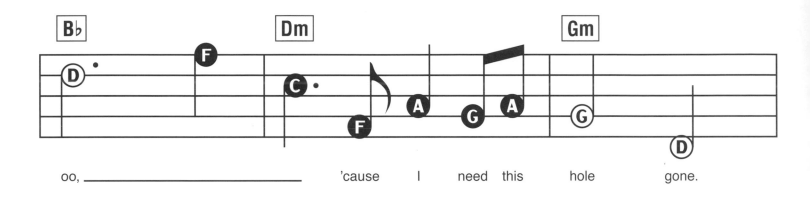

oo, _____ 'cause I need this hole gone.

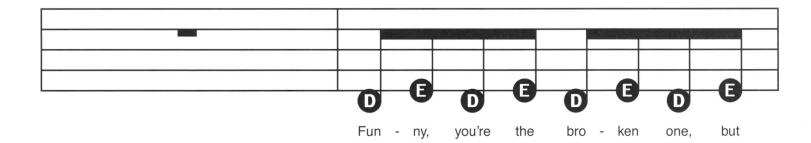

Fun - ny, you're the bro - ken one, but

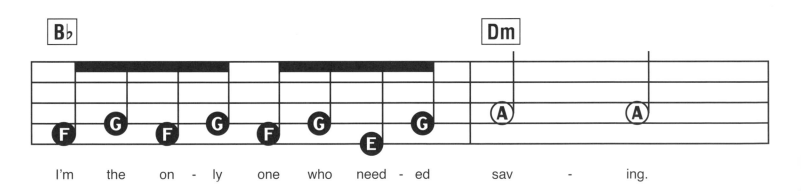

I'm the on - ly one who need - ed sav - ing.

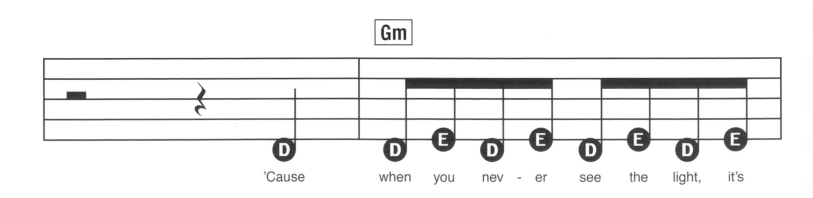

'Cause when you nev - er see the light, it's

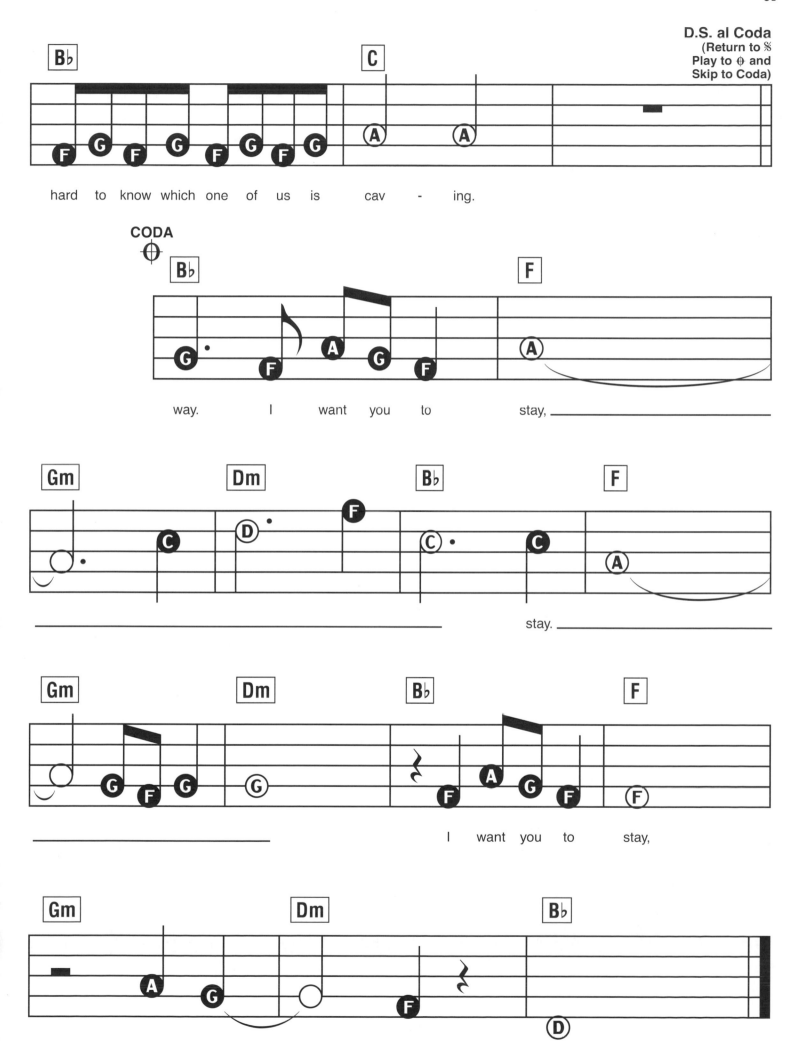

D.S. al Coda
(Return to 𝄋
Play to ⊕ and
Skip to Coda)

Stay with Me

Registration 2
Rhythm: Ballad

Words and Music by Sam Smith,
James Napier and William Edward Phillips

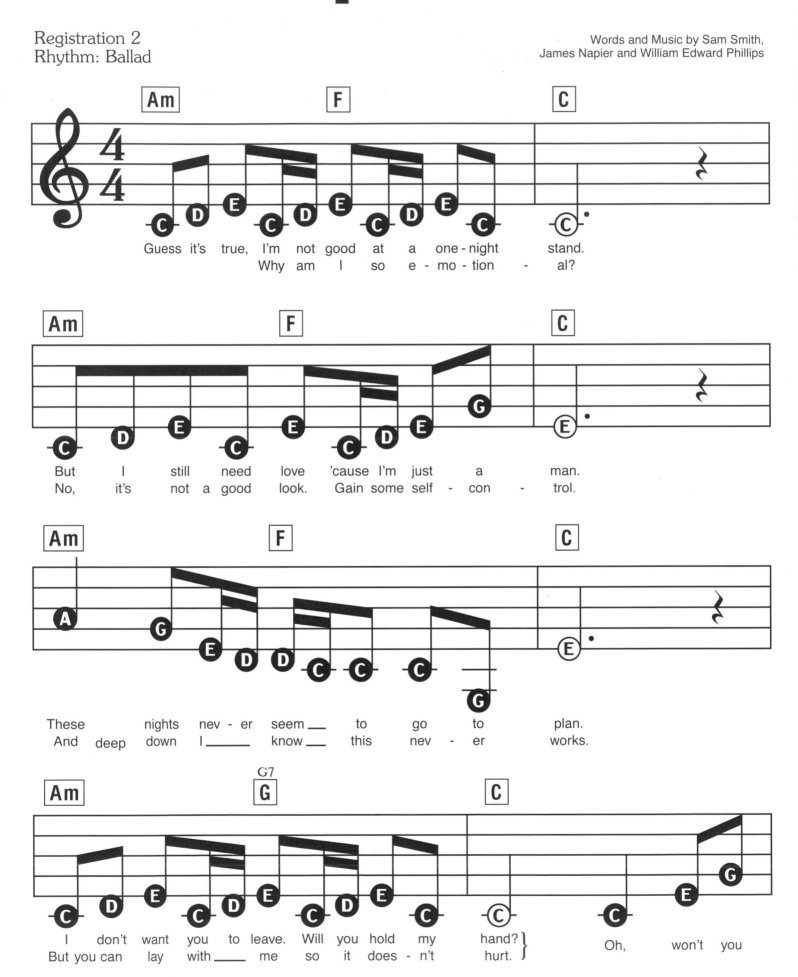

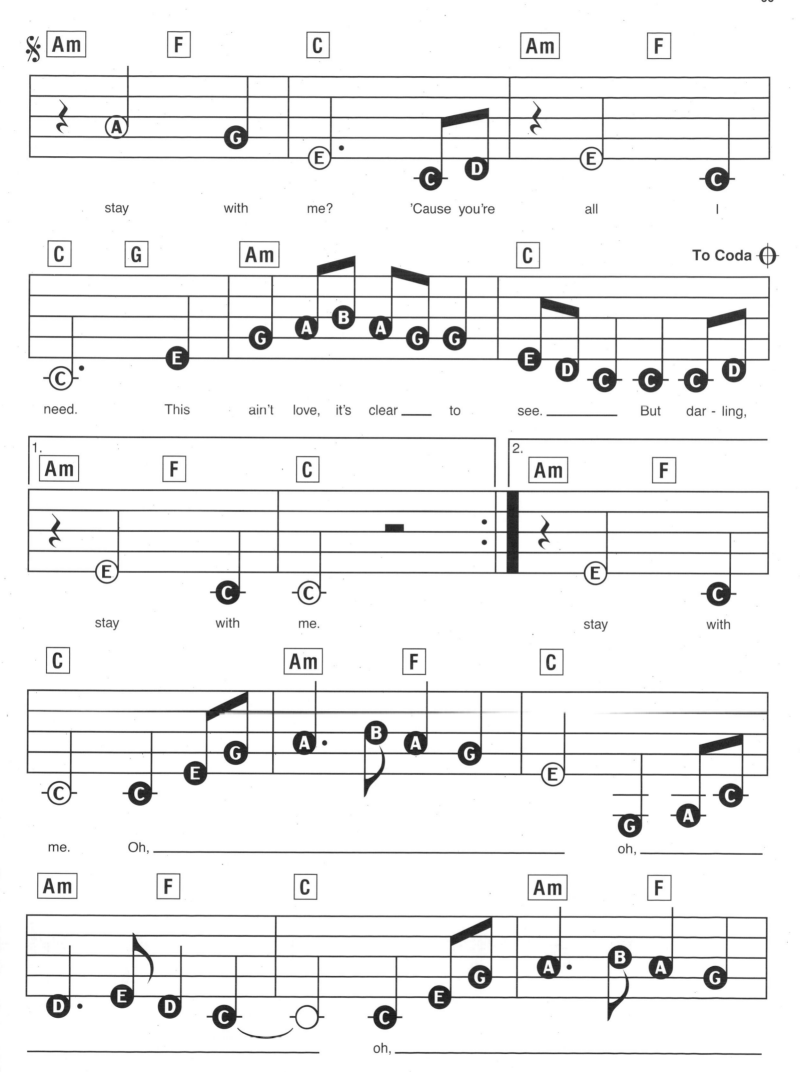

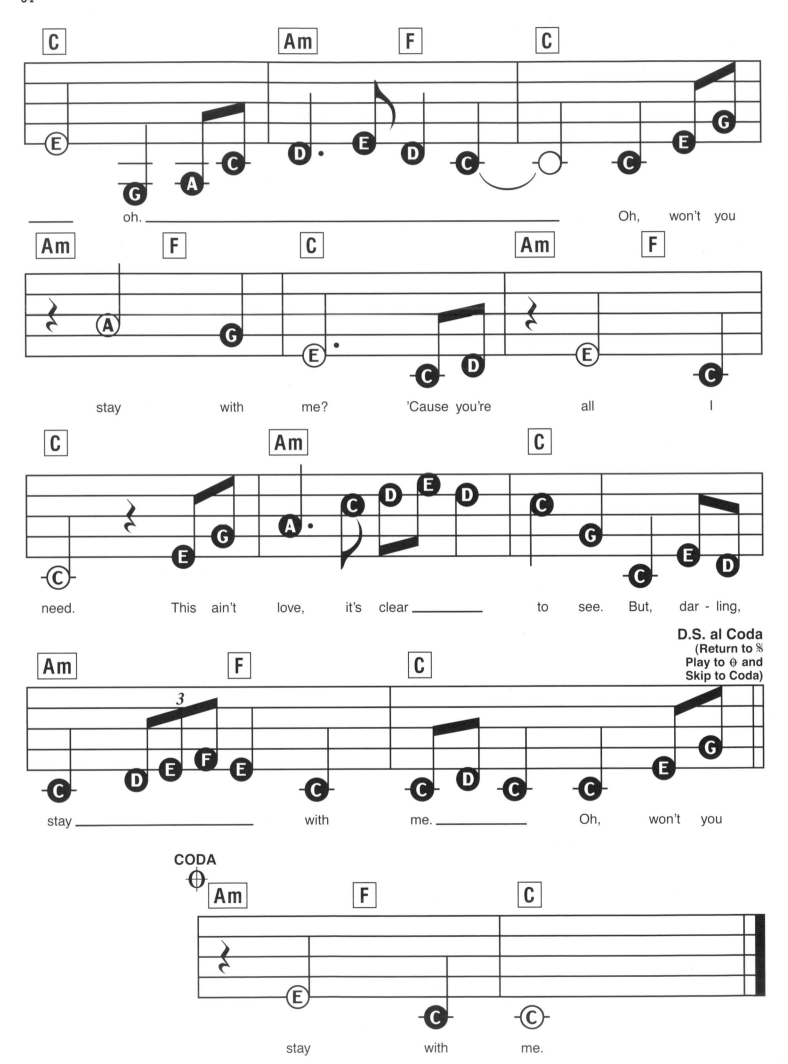

Story of My Life

Registration 4
Rhythm: Folk or Rock

Words and Music by Jamie Scott,
John Henry Ryan, Julian Bunetta,
Harry Styles, Liam Payne,
Louis Tomlinson, Niall Horan
and Zain Malik

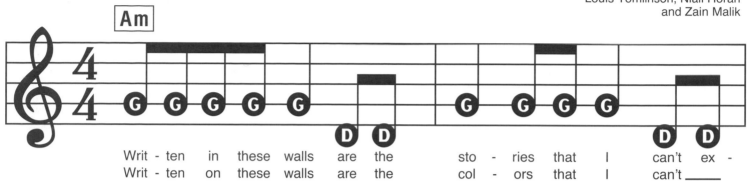

Writ - ten in these walls are the sto - ries that I can't ex -
Writ - ten on these walls are the col - ors that I can't

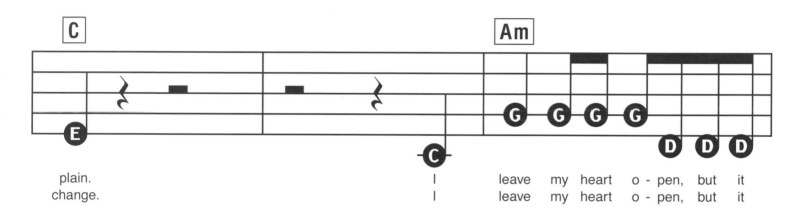

plain. I leave my heart o - pen, but it
change. I leave my heart o - pen, but it

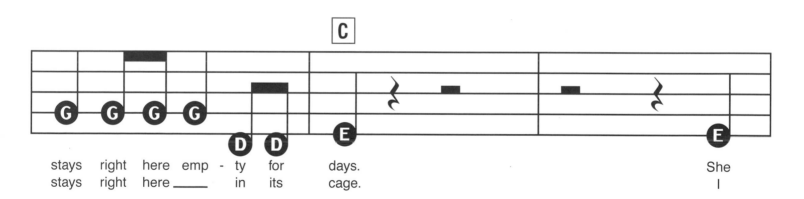

stays right here emp - ty for days. She
stays right here in its cage. I

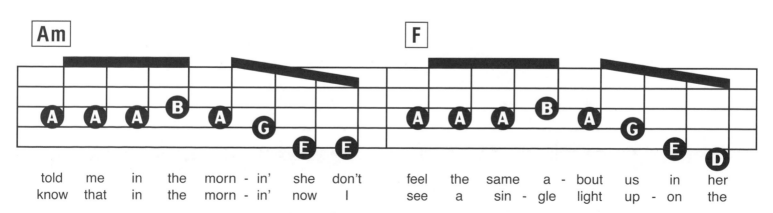

told me in the morn - in' she don't feel the same a - bout us in her
know that in the morn - in' now I see a sin - gle light up - on the

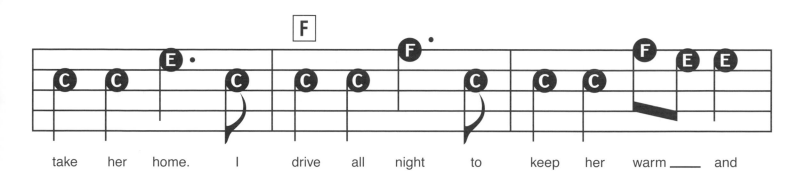

take her home. I drive all night to keep her warm ___ and

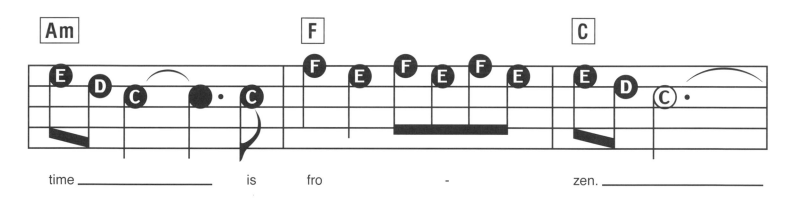

time _____ is fro - zen. _____

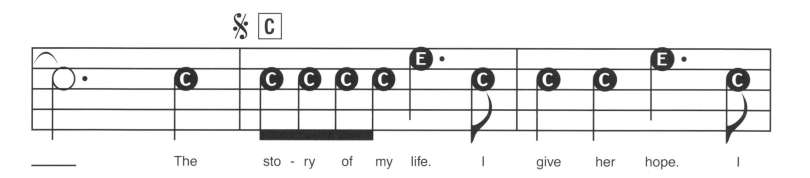

___ The sto - ry of my life. I give her hope. I

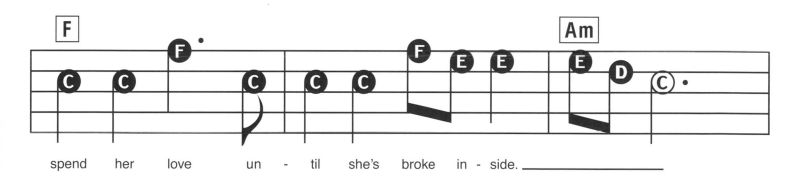

spend her love un - til she's broke in - side. _____

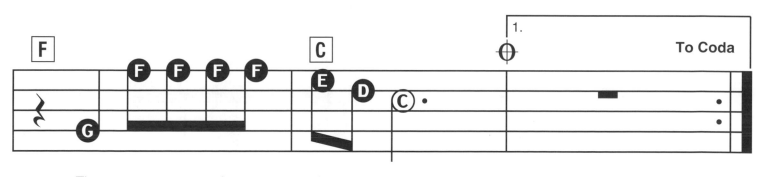

The sto - ry of my life. ___

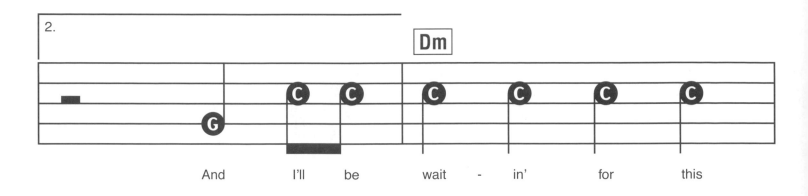

2.

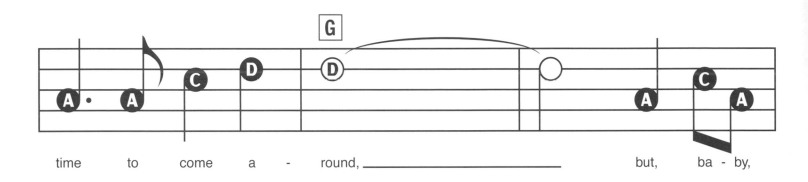

And I'll be wait - in' for this

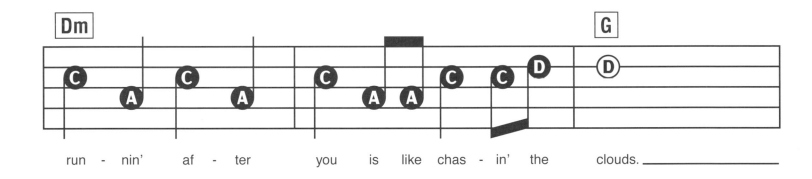

time to come a - round, but, ba - by,

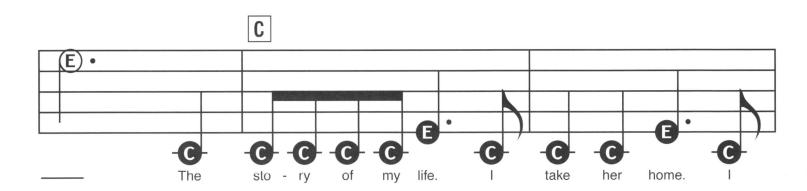

run - nin' af - ter you is like chas - in' the clouds.

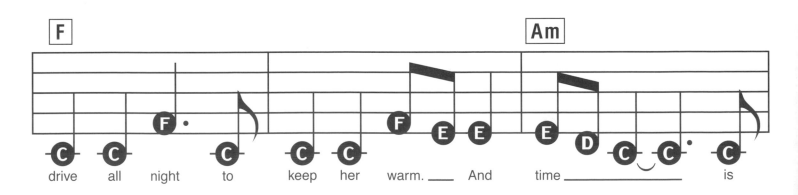

The sto - ry of my life. I take her home. I

drive all night to keep her warm. And time is

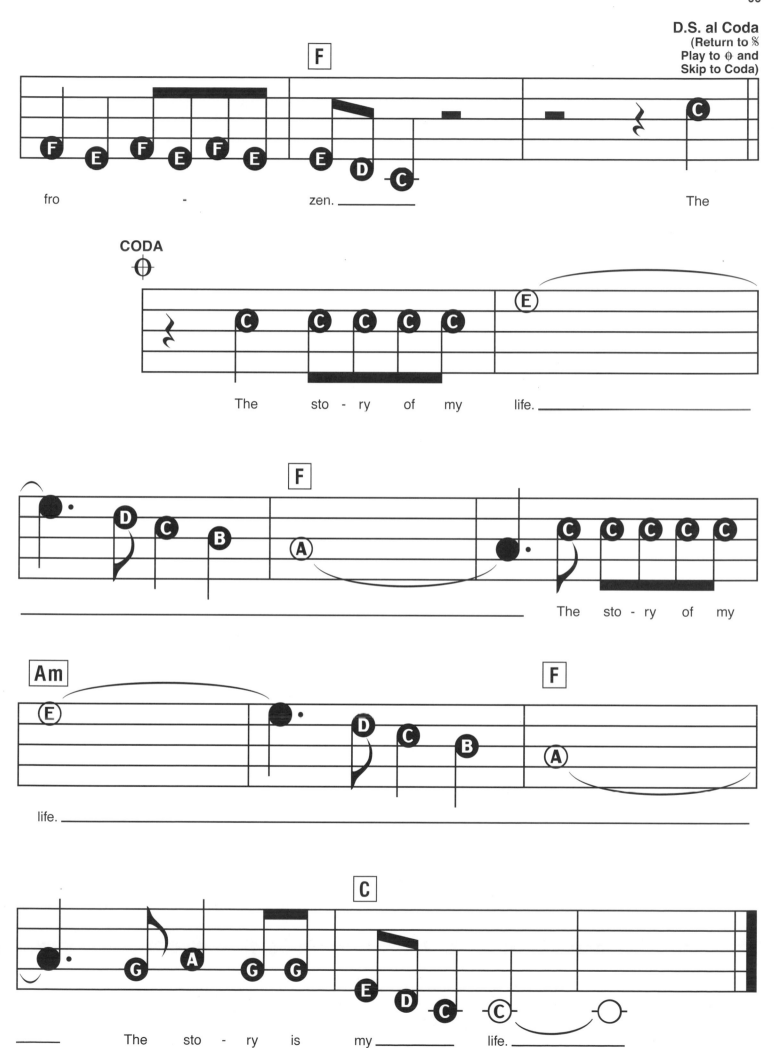

When I Was Your Man

Registration 8
Rhythm: 4/4 Ballad

Words and Music by Bruno Mars,
Ari Levine, Philip Lawrence
and Andrew Wyatt

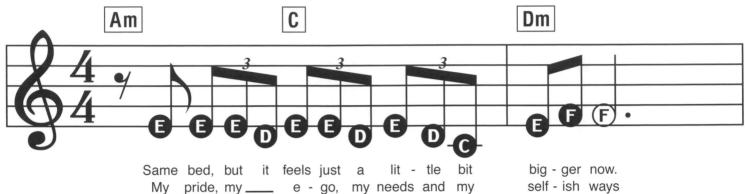

Same bed, but it feels just a lit - tle bit big - ger now.
My pride, my ___ e - go, my needs and my self - ish ways

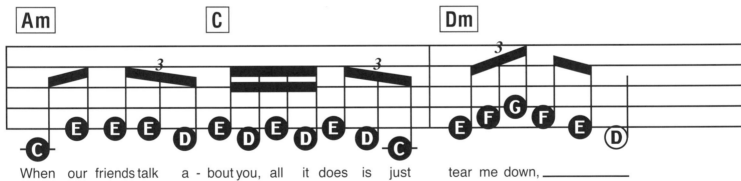

Our song on the ra - di - o, but it don't sound the same.
caused a good strong ___ wom - an like you to walk out my life.

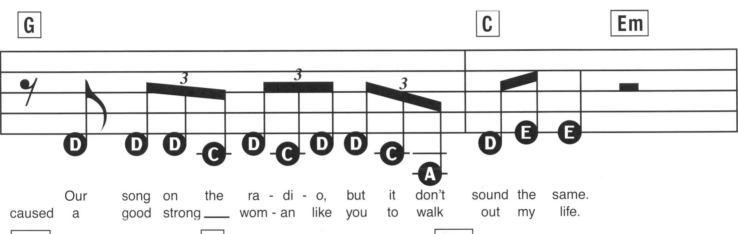

When our friends talk a - bout you, all it does is just tear me down, ___
Now I ___ nev - er get to clean up the mess I've made, ___

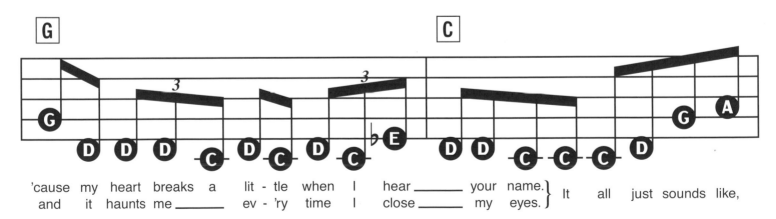

'cause my heart breaks a lit - tle when I hear ___ your name. } It all just sounds like,
and it haunts me ___ ev - 'ry time I close ___ my eyes.

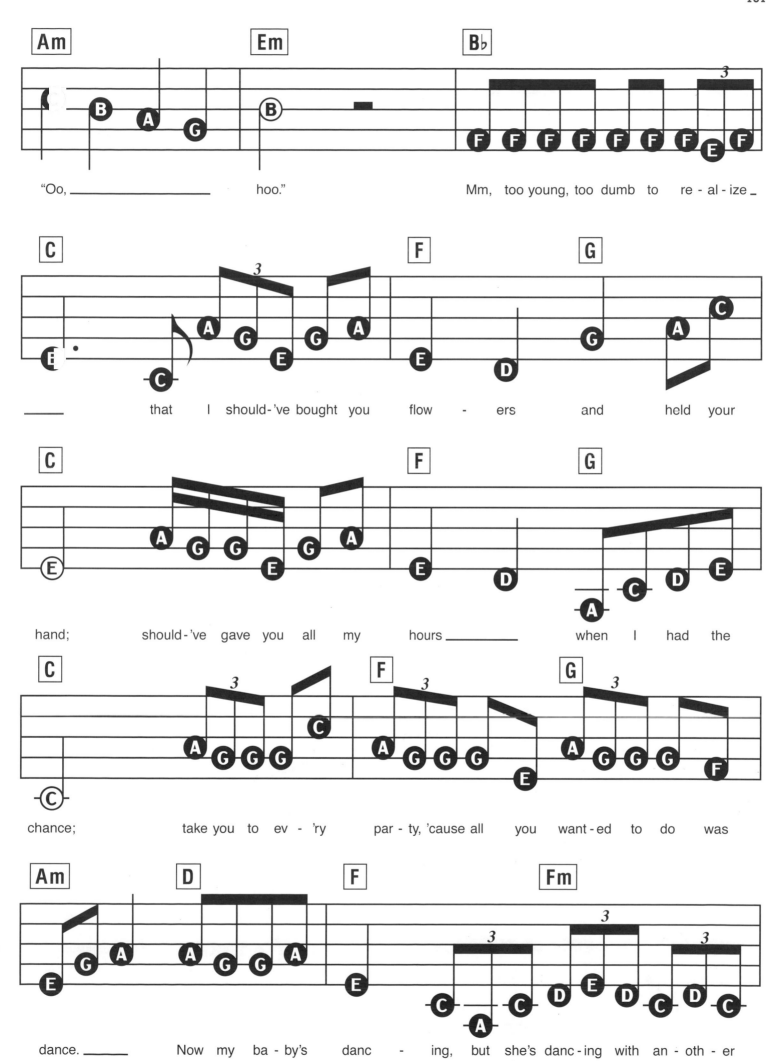

A Thousand Years
from the Summit Entertainment film
THE TWILIGHT SAGA: BREAKING DAWN - Part 1

Registration 8
Rhythm: Waltz

Words and Music by David Hodges
and Christina Perri

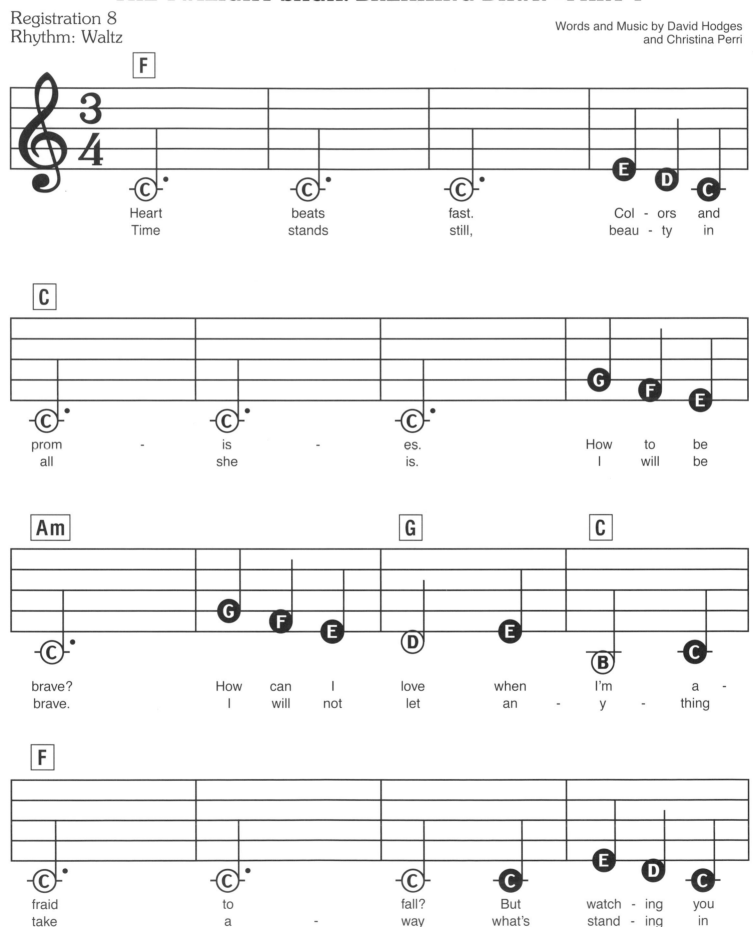

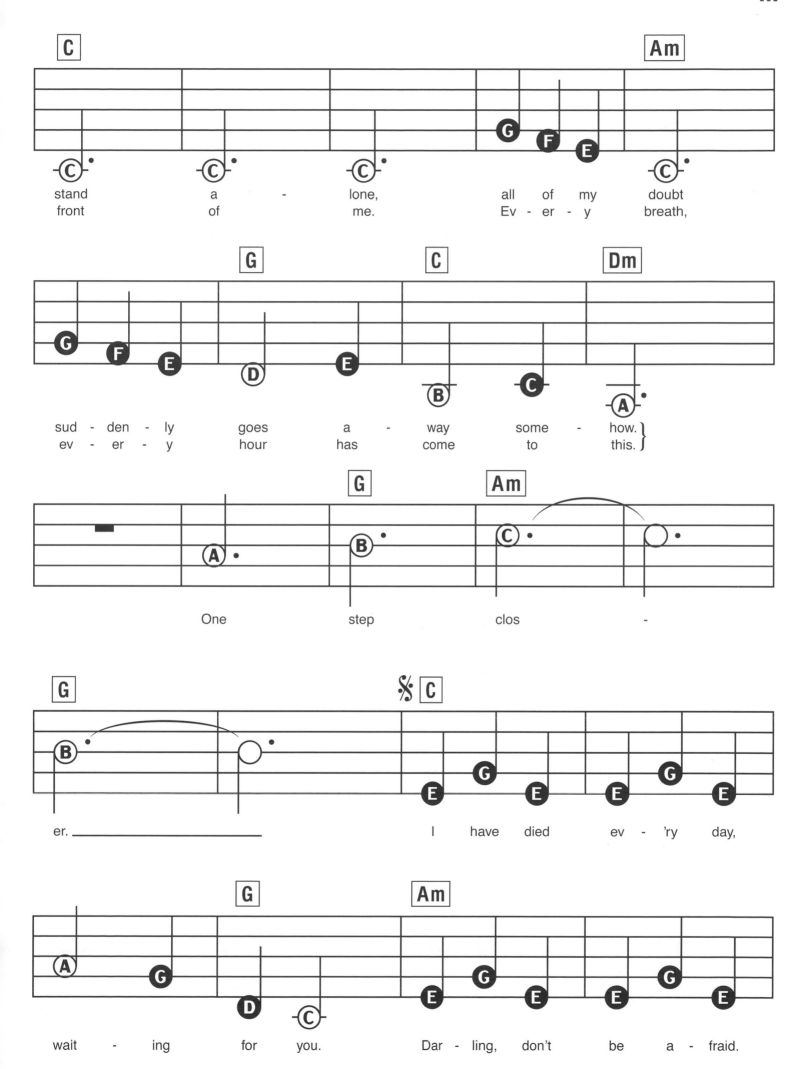

106

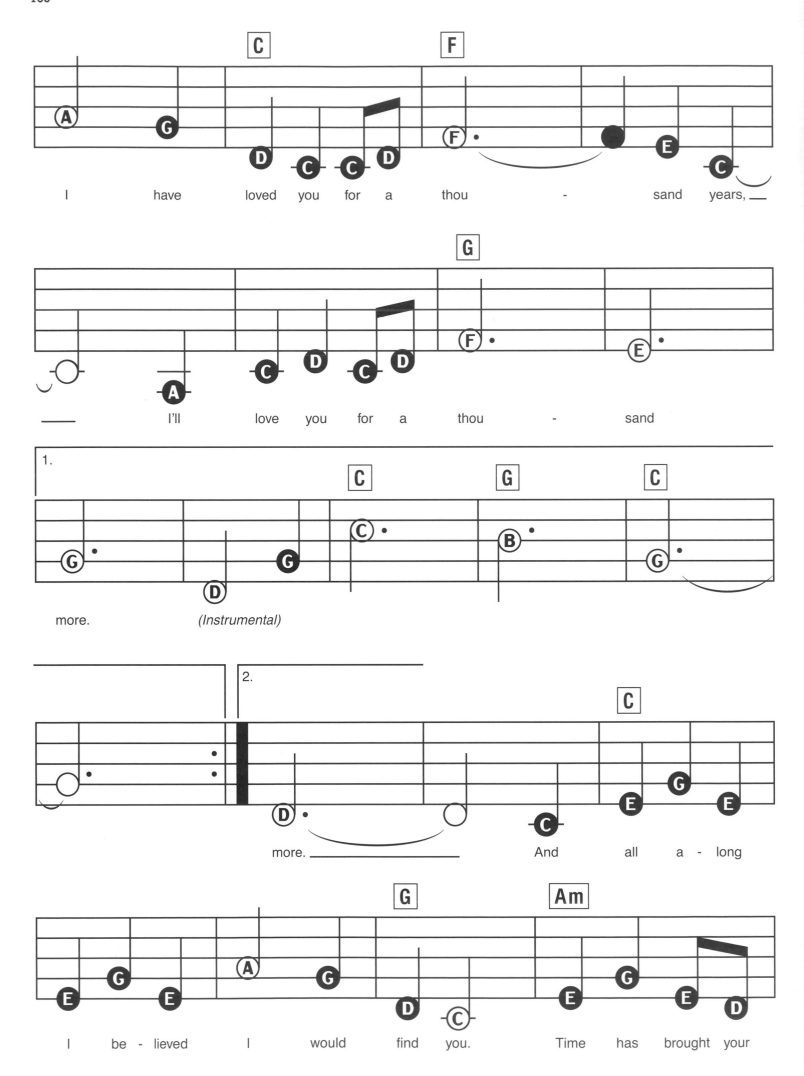

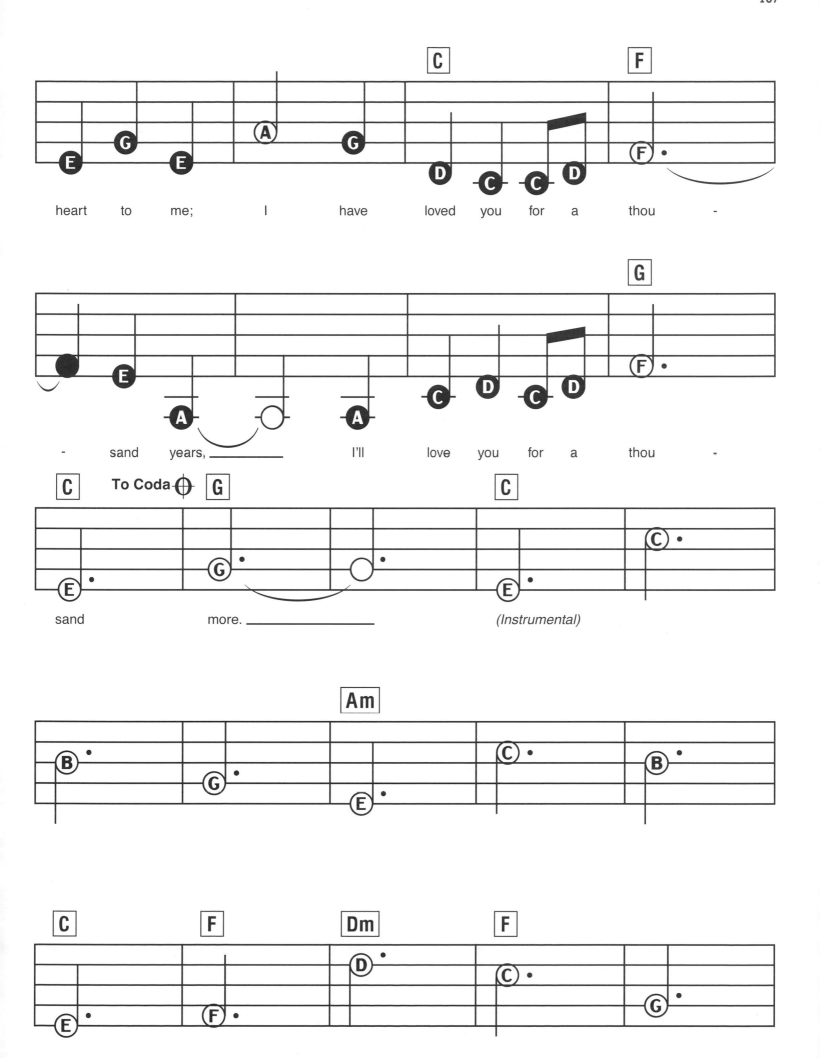

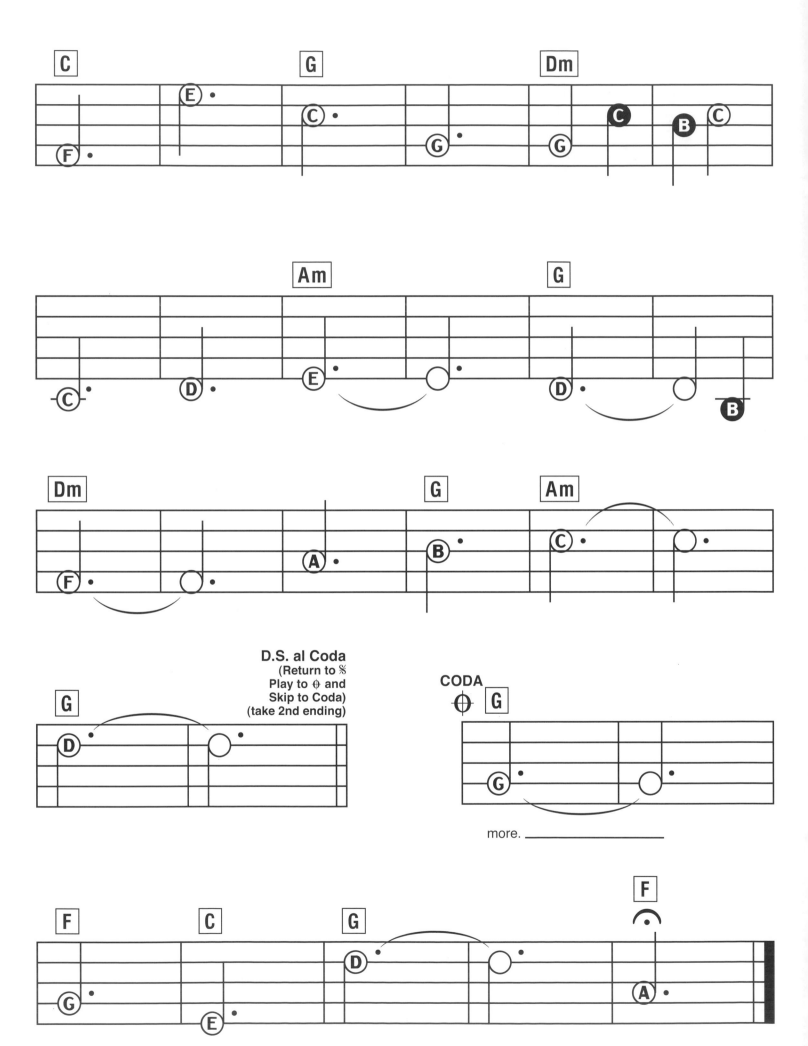

(Instrumental)

Registration Guide

- Match the Registration number on the song to the corresponding numbered category below. Select and activate an instrumental sound available on your instrument.

- Choose an automatic rhythm appropriate to the mood and style of the song. (Consult your Owner's Guide for proper operation of automatic rhythm features.)

- Adjust the tempo and volume controls to comfortable settings.

Registration

1	Mellow	Flutes, Clarinet, Oboe, Flugel Horn, Trombone, French Horn, Organ Flutes
2	Ensemble	Brass Section, Sax Section, Wind Ensemble, Full Organ, Theater Organ
3	Strings	Violin, Viola, Cello, Fiddle, String Ensemble, Pizzicato, Organ Strings
4	Guitars	Acoustic/Electric Guitars, Banjo, Mandolin, Dulcimer, Ukulele, Hawaiian Guitar
5	Mallets	Vibraphone, Marimba, Xylophone, Steel Drums, Bells, Celesta, Chimes
6	Liturgical	Pipe Organ, Hand Bells, Vocal Ensemble, Choir, Organ Flutes
7	Bright	Saxophones, Trumpet, Mute Trumpet, Synth Leads, Jazz/Gospel Organs
8	Piano	Piano, Electric Piano, Honky Tonk Piano, Harpsichord, Clavi
9	Novelty	Melodic Percussion, Wah Trumpet, Synth, Whistle, Kazoo, Perc. Organ
10	Bellows	Accordion, French Accordion, Mussette, Harmonica, Pump Organ, Bagpipes